AUG 4 2015

SPRINGDALE PUBLIC LIBRARY
405 S. Pleasant
Springdale, AR 72764

**A BEGINNING SCULPTOR**

# The Making of a Sculptor

## The Life and Works of Mac Hornecker

**By Marie Hornecker**

Many thanks and love go to Mac's sister, Mary Ann, for the countless hours of telling Mac's early history and her remarkable memory.

To Med, Melissa, and Marcy, whom Mac thought were his greatest accomplishments

To his grandsons, Drew, Maclain, and Noah, who gave him so much joy and pleasure, teaching them to fish and experiencing new adventures.

To Mac's dad, Gordon, and also his aunts and uncles that are now with Mac continuing to take care of him as they did, because it took a village.

# The Making of a Sculptor

## The Life and Works of Mac Hornecker

# CONTENT

**Dedication** - III

**Content** - V

**Prologue** - VI

**Introduction** - VII

**One - Sheldon Missouri 1943** - 1

**Two - Parents** - 19

**Three - College** - 31

**Four - Mac and Marie** - 35

**Five - Kansas City and the Kansas City Art Institute** - 43

**Six - University of Oklahoma and Mac's MFA** - 57

**Seven - Buena Vista College** - 65
     **(Buena Vista University)**

**Eight - Arkadelphia, Arkansas** - 133

**Additional 'Mac Stories'** - 173

**Resume** - 189

**Index of Works** - 194

Cover photo by Dick Hakes

# PROLOGUE

This is the life story of Mac Hornecker - husband, father, brother, teacher, and professional sculptor. The rolling hills of southwest Missouri, where he grew up, formed his personality and interests. He saw all those around him as interesting and happy characters with unique personalities, instead of poor, unorganized, and lazy, as many would have seen them. Many saw the rocky land as poor, but Mac saw it as a landscape canvas, influenced by the glaciers, wind, rain, and the effects of man. His work was always influenced by the rocks, hills, valleys, rocky bluffs, and streams that he knew and grew up around, from southern Missouri to northwest Iowa. Most of his work emerges from the earth, with boulders that look as if they are as much below the ground as above, and tied to the earth, or with geometric shapes that suggest the elements of nature such as wind, or that man is part of the equation as a shaper and builder. His work evolved to be more lyrical with curving lines, not reproducing the landscape, but using it as the "essence".

On many evenings, Mac and his friends and family would sit around telling stories and reminisce and entertain. Mac, in the 1980's, wrote down many of these stories which were found after his death. The included MAC STORIES are just as he wrote them down, so he gets credit for a large part of the writing of this book. Some of these stories are included along with the narrative, and an additional selection can be found at the end of the book.

Mac's introduction to his stories is also a wonderful introduction to the beginning of this book and **what made Mac 'Mac'**.

## Mac Stories

## Introduction
**By Mac Hornecker**

This was the time, before television, when people had the opportunity to establish their ways without many outside influences.  They lived in small pocket communities, usually located around a one room school.  Their connection with the outside world came from pie suppers and other activities, usually held at the schoolhouse.  Once in a while they would go on a one-day trip somewhere, but they had to be back in time to do the milking.  Milking, which needed to be done twice a day, kept their lives very stable.  They had a radio, powered by a battery and, oh yes, the crank wall type telephone with numbers like two longs and a short, or three longs, or two shorts.

 These people had the same basic economic base, which was just enough to get by from the egg and milk check.  They grew and canned all their food, butchered a hog in the fall, cured the meat, and lived the good life with gravy for every meal.  They worked hard, but not too hard.  They liked to fish and hunt and tell stories, and they talked about the weather a lot.  Any spare time was spent doing creative things like sewing, cutting wood, and building stuff, and they made some very good things.  They enjoyed the old ways and were slow to change until TV appeared on the scene.

 At any rate, great characters and legends developed in these communities.  These people and families provided entertainment for all the people including those in the surrounding communities.  Stories about these people were passed around from person to person and were their main source of entertainment.  The stories usually ended with humor or a moral, usually one and the same.

# ONE

## SHELDON, MISSOURI

### April 10, 1943

**W**ell, this is where it all started, Hornecker Hospital, Sheldon, Missouri, on April 10, 1943. One might think that Hornecker Hospital was the small town hospital of a Dr. Hornecker, but then you wouldn't understand rural southwest Missouri. Hornecker Hospital was the house of Aunt Effie and Uncle Earn Hornecker. As you entered the front door, there were two rooms to the left. The first held a "birthing table" and the back room held three beds. It is documented, in Aunt Effie's log, over twelve hundred babies were born at Hornecker Hospital by this self-proclaimed midwife, and sometimes a doctor, if there was a doctor in the area, and if he happened to be in town.

This was the beginning of a sculptor in a place that had no idea what the word "sculpture" meant. These were poor, hard-working people, trying to live and farm on marginal land of rolling hills, hollers, ravines, small streams, and rocky bluffs. Sheldon was, and still is, a small town of about 500 people, 12 miles south of the bigger town of Nevada, Missouri, on Highway 71, in the southwest part of the state.

There were several large families in the area with some having up to 12 children. Many times several members of one family would marry siblings from another family. Anyone entering the family from outside the area had a big job trying to figure out who was related to whom, but mostly, at that time, there were the Horneckers, Cliffmans, and Gordons. Many may have been poor but they enjoyed life and felt like they were just one big family.

In the early summer of '42, a year before Mac was born, the kerosene cooking stove in the farmhouse Mac's family was renting, caught on fire and burned the house to the ground. Gordon, Mac's dad, was in the field and saw smoke but couldn't get to it in time. Luckily no one was hurt. For the next three to four months, the family lived in a canvas army tent with a dirt floor, while a new house was being built on the same spot. An old house from the Wild Rose community was torn down and the boards were used to build the new house.

They slept and lived in the tent and cooked in the smokehouse on a wood stove. Of course the "Family Village" jumped into action and soon the girls were wearing new handmade clothes, mostly out of flour and feed sacks. In those days, chicken feed came in cotton sacks, not like the gunny sacks with color and print on them. When the feed was gone, women used the sacks to make all kinds of things. Four sacks sewn together made perfect bed sheets; match the pattern and make a dress, or make anything from curtains to dish towels.

Mac was the third child of Pauline and Gordon Hornecker. Bonnie was ten and Mary Ann was six when Mac was born. Mac was lucky to be born in Hornecker Hospital, because Mary Ann was born in their farm house. Gordon was in the field trying to finish up the haying but little Mary Ann just couldn't wait.

Mac, as he was known by everyone, was actually Edward Mac Arthur Hornecker - four names, not MacArthur. It so happened he was named after two grandfathers, Edward and Arthur, and his dad wanted to name him Mac, so everyone was happy.

Nine months after Mac was born, his mother Pauline, died of kidney stones; at least that is the best guess they had at the time. Many people thought Gordon should give up the children, but he adamantly refused. One family wanted Mary Ann so their daughter, an only child, would have a playmate. And of course, there was the worry that some would want the children so they would have more people to work in the fields. The practice of adopting for that reason was not unheard of during those times and had happened in their neighborhood.

Again the "Family Village" helped Gordon raise his family. His sister, Helen, had a son just a few months younger, so Mac went down the road to Aunt Helen's during the week when the girls would be in school, and then went home on the weekends.

It was pretty challenging for those two girls to take care of a baby, especially without inside plumbing. Aunt Helen would get the diaper rash just about cleared up, when it was time for Mac to go home for the weekend. When he would come back on Monday, Aunt Helen had to start all over.

When Mac got to be about three years old, most of the time he would stay in the house by himself while Gordon was working in the fields, tending the livestock, and milking the cows. While he was home alone, he would experience the world of creativity. He would draw and make art and would have to be clever to find materials to work with, a trait that carried him through all the lean years of his professional career. Sometimes he would tear out the red horses from the Mobil Oil ads. He was so proud of his horse collection and get so mad when they would be thrown away when the house was cleaned.

There was never money for store bought toys. Gordon would make homemade toys like a "squirrel on a stick". That was a great toy with a coat hanger inside a groove cut into the side of the stick, attached to a whittled out squirrel with jointed legs. You would pull and push the wire so the squirrel would run up and down the stick. Now you know, where this sculptor got his creativity.

In the spring of '48 the house, which belonged to an aunt and uncle, was sold. It was thought to have been sold to help their son set up his car agency in the nearby town of Lamar. The son also went on to become the Mayor. After World War II there was a demand for farmland. One reason, was because of a farm program to train veterans, with a stipend for participation. It was a returning GI that bought the farm.

Mac's family then moved about four miles to the Longacre community. Mac's dad bought the little 120-acre farm, for about $1200. This was Mac's final home until he went to college. This old house was pretty black inside and out, like a dungeon and filthy besides, as a one-armed man had lived there. Thinking back, it had to be pretty tough to provide for himself, or even make fires, and he was way out in the country without a car. The front part had been a little two room house, and the back two rooms, which became bedrooms, had been an old corn crib. This was a pretty primitive home, as many were.

They moved to the new place in a wagon with two horses, as Mary Ann amazingly recalls, that were named Daisy and Maude. Mary Ann rode on the load with one of their uncles, and they moved everything in one day. Another uncle papered one of the bedrooms and two aunts swept everything from the ceiling down. By night time, they were all settled in and milking went on as usual. The only thing better, at the new house, was that they had a pump, rather than a draw bucket, to get water from the well. They could sit in the living room, but the wallpaper was hanging from the ceiling almost to the floor. It stayed that way for a while, because the roof leaked and the roof and ceiling plaster had to be fixed, before the room could be papered.

After fixing it up, the house had just four rooms; a living room, kitchen, and two bedrooms and a back screen porch. It was heated with a wood stove in the living room and did not have any inside plumbing. A big water bucket was on a stand in the kitchen and an outhouse was in the side yard, a "two holler", no less. Baths were taken in the living room by the wood stove in the wintertime and on the back porch in the summer. They were taken in a big wash tub, one person right after the other. The water was heated on the wood stove and there was a pecking order and lineup of who got to take a bath first and get the hottest, cleanest water.

The Horneckers always ate pretty well, but had some of the same things over and over because they ate what they grew or canned. They usually butchered a hog and had it cut up and hanging in the smokehouse, along with chickens they raised for meat and eggs. Gord wouldn't let them eat a chicken until it weighed three pounds, so when the chickens started to get bigger, the kids were constantly running them down and setting them on a scale, anxiously waiting for that needle to point to 3.

Of course, they also hunted for some of their food. The best was fried squirrel with biscuits and squirrel gravy. When Mac's sister, Mary Ann, was just 10 years old, she would shoot a squirrel, skin it, and then cook it for dinner. Of course you always had to shoot the squirrel in the head so you wouldn't ruin the meat. When she got to high school she wished she could have gone out for the rifle team. They weren't use to girls being so good at precision shooting, but a moving squirrel's head, was harder to hit than any bullseye target.

Mac had so many stories about the interesting times when he grew up, about members of his family and characters of the area. When he would get together with his childhood friends, they would all chime in with the stories, and they would laugh harder than anyone, and sometimes added a lot of embellishments, depending on the crowd. Here are some 'MAC STORIES' about butchering hogs and other food delicacies in their life.

A 'Mac Story' #1

## SHOT HOG

In those days people butchered their own meat. Where we lived most people ate more pork than anything else. They sugar-cured and smoked the meat.

Homemade sausage was real good. When they cut up the hog, all meat scraps went into the bathtub; the round #2 we used to take baths by the stove in the winter and on the back porch in the summer. We had a hand grinder bolted to a table leaf that would sit on two five-gallon lard cans.

Dad would add pepper, black and red, and sage to the meat scraps and grind it up into sausage. He would sit on one end of the table leaf and use one of us kids on the other end to hold it down on the lard cans. Sweat would roll off Dad out there in the old smokehouse, but of course we kids would be freezing just sitting on the can.

In another tub, all of the fat scraps were thrown and would later be rendered into lard. For this we used a big cast-iron kettle set up on three rocks. We would throw in the fat and build a fire around the outside of the kettle. This made a neat smell. Sometimes when the lard was almost done and the grease was hot, we would cook homemade doughnuts, dip them out and throw them in a paper sack with sugar and shake. Now that was some real eatin'.

Well, one fall day it was time to butcher. A whole bunch of relatives and neighbors went together that year. We were going to butcher five hogs. Of course, it would start raining that day but we were set. My uncle had a vat made out of tin, for water to scald the hogs. We had a hay frame, off of the wagon wheels, sitting on the ground next to the vat. We used log chains to go around the hog so it could be rolled around in the hot water and then pulled up onto the hay frame to be scraped. This was a slick operation. After the hog was scraped, it was hung in a tree by the back legs with a 'single tree'. My dad would gut it and then saw down the backbone to split it in half. Then each person would take his hog home to his smokehouse to cut it up into chops, hams, bacon, sausage, lard, and whatever else they made. Some pickled the feet and ears. Some used the tail for a pot of beans. They used to say that we used everything but the SQUEAL...

Our hog was the last of the five. We had to drive about three miles up to our house to get it. We were going to shoot him right between the eyes and my uncle was going to 'stick' him.

The hog was lying back in the low shed we had, on his belly looking straight at us. My dad had been shooting the hogs, but he handed me the old 22 single shot so I could do the job. I had come of age and was probably about twelve or thirteen. Well, I shot too low and the bullet did not kill him, but he sure came out of the shed with some speed. He went right between my uncle's legs. My uncle was riding the hog backward. They went down over a steep bank, the Jimson Weeds a rattlin'. As they went by me, my Uncle was a ridin' and a stabbin' that hog. It seemed like forever to a frightened kid, but in a second or two my uncle yelled "I GOT HIM!!

I think that was about the last time we butchered at home.

# A 'Mac Story' #2

## PICKLED PIGS PARTS

All the spare pig parts were used to make head cheese; ears, tails, snouts, and the other parts. A lot of people liked to use the tail to make a big pot of beans. Every family had a preference as to how they use these parts.

Our family always pickled these spare parts. Feet, ears, heart, and many other parts went into a gallon glass jar that always sat in the middle of the kitchen table. Most of the houses were small and the only dining table was in the kitchen by the wood cook stove.

Beans and corn bread was a staple. Some folks liked pinto beans, some black eyed peas, but most liked navy beans. For Sunday, sometimes, we'd have butter beans.

Rich city relatives would come for a visit and be amazed at the great tasting beans with ham hocks, tail, or other parts they never saw in the grocery stores in the city. They were always curious and tried to identify the parts.

After supper my Dad would pull the big jar of pickled pig parts over and unscrew the lid and fish out some parts with a fork. The boys were there from the city and would set and watch and ask, "What part is that?"

It was a good anatomy lesson. They couldn't wait for each night to ask Dad which part he was eating. The next day they would go down to the hog lot and check it out on a live hog.

One night Dad was fishin' out some parts and he got a piece of the ear. The ear had been too big to get in the jar hole so he had cut it up in strips about an inch wide. He had the piece that came right next to the head. Those boys checked it out.

"Round with a wrinkly hole. What part is that?" they ask. Dad, with a big grin, licked his chops and replied, "That's his asshole", and gulped it down like it was the best part ever.

Those city boys had a lot to learn. To this day they make sure they know the anatomy of everything they eat.

## A 'Mac Story' #3

## APPLES

We loved apples. We didn't have an orchard so it was the one thing we usually bought. Each fall, Dad or my uncle would take a pickup to an orchard across the county, or sometimes to Arkansas, and get the back of the truck clear full of apples. I would divide them up when they got home.

We would dig a big pit out in the garden usually fairly close to the outhouse. The pit was lined with straw, and then the apples, and then straw on top. Some gunny sacks were placed around the outside for access, and then the dirt was put on top. These pits were also used to bury turnips and carrots.

Whoever had to go to the outhouse was expected to get some apples for snackin,' on the way back to the house. If snow on the seat of the outhouse wasn't bad enough, lying on your belly reaching in a hole and running your hand through a rotten apple was.

The smell of wood smoke and the fresh hay fed to the cows filled the air, but apples and popcorn around the wood stove was just about the best.

## A 'Mac Story' #4

## COLD SWEET TATERS

The only time we had candy was around Christmas. The other times we mostly had popcorn, peanuts, apples and cold baked sweet taters. We grew them all.

Popcorn we usually kept on the cob in a gunny sack that hung from the rafters by baling wire in the smokehouse. That way the mice couldn't get into it so bad. When we wanted popcorn, someone had to run out to the smokehouse and get a few ears. Then we would all set around and shell it and throw the cobs in the stove. We would then go outside and poured it from pan to pan to let the wind blow out the chaff and any dirt that might be on it, and then popped it in bacon grease. Yumm! Yumm!

Peanuts we kept in gunny sacks in the same way. They were pocket food while we did our chores after school. They also let Dad know what chores were finished by the fresh hulls on the ground.

Apples were great. A lot of times we ate them with the popcorn.

An old neighbor from the old country introduced us to cold sweet taters. We always ate them hot with brown sugar or molasses or baked with butter. He always baked a bunch at a time and laid them up on the top shelf of his wood cook stove.

To us kids, they were like candy bars. You could see us walking around peeling back the skin and learning the old way and about the hard times.

Mac was now five when they made their last move, and he started attending the Longacre one room schoolhouse, and the girls had to leave their Avola schoolhouse behind.   Mac and his sisters went for just a few days before the school year ended for the summer.

Getting to school was not easy but was quite an adventure.  When the girls went to the Avola schoolhouse before they moved, they would have to walk through the timber and cross a pretty big branch, and climb over and through a few fences to get there. They usually just had a foot log which was especially handy when they would have a big rain.  The water would be deep and running fast.  It was a miracle that no one drowned, but they were agile and tough, and had a lot of good sense.

It was amazing how much activity went on during and after school, especially considering that the teachers were so young with little experience.  The room usual consisted of a teacher's desk and a recitation bench, a big old pot belly stove, book shelves and blackboards on the walls, and a piano.  Of course there was a coal bucket and crock water container, which leaked on the floor in the Avola School.  The book shelves would hold a set of World Books, a dictionary, and several reading books, and they would hang curtains up from the shelves for their plays and recitations.  They were wonderful rooms to decorate with crape paper and they would make things in their art classes to decorate the windows.

There would be a well close by, with a pump and a metal cup hanging on it that the students all shared. They did not worry about sanitation.  A flag pole would be in the yard and most every morning the students would line up by grades and pledge allegiance to the flag before school started, or when it was icy, they would have the pledge  inside.  Outside there would be a coal house and two outhouses, one for the boys and one for the girls.   The school was usually situated on a piece of land that had a yard big enough for a place to play 'work up' baseball.  They would also play 'Beacon' in the sedge grass, and in the winter they would play 'Fox and Goose 'and have snowball fights and make forts.  In the Avola school the only playground equipment was a homemade teeter totter until the school finally made enough money to buy a basketball and Gordon made a basketball goal.  The schools were just right for playing 'Handy-Over' and of course ' Hide and Seek', ' Flying Dutchman', ' Mother May I', 'Dodge Ball', and jump rope.   Shooting marbles was one of the most fun things to play and a classmate's mother made Mary Ann a little drawstring bag for her marbles.

Their subjects were Reading, Writing, Arithmetic, Spelling, Art, and Music.  Beginning in the third grade, Geography, History, Science, and Health were added, and the seventh and eighth grades brought Conservation and Farm related subjects.  Now days, one just wonders how those young teachers did it all.

Besides an enormous amount of subjects to teach with such a age range of children, they also would have monthly PTA meetings; pie suppers; Halloween, Christmas, St. Pat's Day, and Valentine's Day parties; and the last day of school parties with parents and families.

School hours were from 9 to 4 and school hardly ever canceled or let out early.  The kids were tough and walked in whatever obstacle the weather handed them.

There were usually about 20 kids in 8 grades and the teacher was usually pretty strict.  Mary Ann remembered one day that the only classmate in her grade, got a lickin' for blowing his ink on the back of his

Big Chief Tablet. He was making artful designs and in hindsight, Mary Ann thinks he was just ahead on both, good uses for ink and modern art.

The teachers had to be pretty creative and so energetic to be able to work with so few supplies and 8 grades. At the Avola school, when it was hot, the teacher would take them down to the creek and use gunny sacks to seine for crawdads, and give oral reports while baking potatoes wrapped in mud in their campfire. Of course they ate plenty of raw potatoes but no one complained. Sometimes a mother would come with an old truck and the students would just all pile into the back and go to another school to play with other kids. There was never any worry about liability in those days.

When they moved and had to switch to the Longacre schoolhouse, it was a lot different. There were no marble players there but they did have a commercial swing set. This teacher had an ailing sister who she brought to school with her every day, and the sister just laid on a cot. The teacher spent most of her time with her sister, and the students never did have a clue what was wrong with her.

The kids would put their lunches up in the cold windowsills in the wintertime to keep them cold and the Jell-O would be set for lunch. Some of the kids were well off enough to have a bologna sandwich which was the envy of many of the others. Mac often had gravy sandwiches, which he thought were pretty good. His sister remembers seeing one of the boys peeling an orange and thought, "how did he get so lucky to have an orange".

As was the custom then, the teacher would have graduated from high school and gone to 'college' for three months during the summer, before she started teaching. The one room school was a great experience for those who had a yearning to learn, because you could be learning at any grade level if you just paid attention. Also, the older students would need to help the younger students, which would reinforce what they had learned. While in the third grade, which consisted of three students, Mac and his friend George picked on the other third grader. Well as the story goes, the other student was the teacher's pet, so she up and flunked both Mac and George; or through the years, that is the way Mac and George remember it.

They did have a lot of fun at their Longacre schoolhouse although Mac's sister thought the kids at Longacre School were meaner than at their old Avola school. Avola people were more fun loving and did things to cause a good laugh, while Longacre kids did a lot of picking on one another...speech, clothing, actions, smartness, dumbness, and such...probably bullying by today's standards.

Like all kids, they were always pulling pranks. One day at noon they filled the boys old pit toilet with sedge grass and then just as school took up for the afternoon, someone set it on fire, and smoke came boiling out of the little vent. School was disrupted and they were finally let out to go home. Another time, someone brought a bunch of garlic from home and they put it in the well. The teacher dismissed school so no one would get sick. Well, they decided to walk about four miles up to Bethel School to say "Hi". By the time they walked back to their Longacre School and then home another two miles or so, they had cooled off. It was hard to tell who was dumber, the kids or the teacher. They tried smoking fairly often. They tried tablet paper, but it burned their throats all the way down, and smoking grapevines could burn a little too.

One day, one little innocent girl brought real rolled cigarettes and a lot of cigarette butts, and the Hagerman kids had a big supply of some kind of little reed they were pulling from an old chair, which was very good tasting. A lot of activity went on in those old outhouses but no one remembers anyone getting hurt or destroying anything, just working off steam and orneriness.

## A 'Mac Story' # 5

## GRAPEVINES

Have you every smoked a grapevine? You use a dead one that is dry and use the sections between the joints. Corn silks are good too, but grapevines are better 'cause you don't need any paper.

There were wild possum grapes vines about anywhere you looked. Persimmon trees in the fence rows always seemed to be a good place to find vines. On those walks back and forth to school, kids need something to do, other than having the girls hitting the boys over the head with their lunch pails, so you could get a persimmon for a snack and a grapevine for a smoke at the same time.

There is no way to explain the flavor of grapevine smoke. It smells and tastes a lot like incense.

We always liked to break in a new kid or someone from town. They were always leery of us anyway, probably for good reason. Anyway, grapevines were a good smoke and you looked so nifty walking along with a grey haze. Girls smoked too. The secret was to smoke slowly, but the new kids always went to fast, just to prove themselves. The next day however, their tongues felt like they had been peeled.

There is always a price for trying to be cool.


When the one room schoolhouse closed, Mac started to school in Nevada, Missouri for his fourth grade. Mac's house was right on the line between Sheldon, with the population of 500, and Nevada, with a population of around 10,000. Going to Nevada gave Mac and his youngest sister, Mary Ann, the opportunity for a much better education.

By the time Mac was eleven years old, Mary Ann was 17, had just graduated, and was leaving for college at the University of Missouri, to be a nurse. His older sister Bonnie had gotten married right after graduating from high school, and lived on a farm nearby. Now, Mac and his dad were bachelors and lived the bachelor life. It would be a dream come true, to have a great deal of freedom at that age, if it weren't for needing to do the chores; be there to milk the cows before school in time to catch the bus; and milk again in the evenings. Mac always took Physical Education or PE as a first class so he could shower and cleanup at school, which was quite a bit above heating the water and bathing in the big wash tub beside the wood stove. Of course there were always other chores; watermelons patches to hoe, haying in the fall and summer, sprouts to spray, and helping his Dad with his many 'jack-of-all trades' jobs. Mac actually could have come home at any hour if he thought he could have done the jobs around the farm the next day, without being miserable.

One day Mac came home in the wee hours of the morning. Gord called him to get outside and start to work, but he didn't come. So, Gord went up to the bedroom window and with his hands cupped around his mouth, yelled close to the glass. It shattered before Gord's eyes. Mac was up and at the milking barn before he knew what hit him.

When he was smaller he knew when he was in trouble. Instead of an ass whipin' he would get an ass kickin'. Mac may have exaggerated a little, but Gord would grab hold of his arm and kick his ass with the side of his foot many times as they went round and round in a circle. Mac and his dad actually were a great team and friends with a lot of mutual respect. 'A Mac Story' about the Tree Frog shows the simple fun times they shared.

## A 'Mac Story' # 6

# Tree Frog

Baseball had been a big event in our neighborhood. There were ball diamonds in every little town and still quite a few in cow pastures. There were makeshift ball teams that would get together and play on Sunday afternoons. A lot of these cow pasture players went on to play in the big leagues. This all ended with organized baseball and television.

That was about it for sports except huntin' and fishin'. Out of necessity these two had almost become professional, for if you weren't good at them you might not have anything to eat.

Oh, there were other sports like teasing the cat, scaring the chickens, or riding the boar hog, but one of the oldest was feedin' the frog.

Dad and I lived like 2 bachelors and lived in an old house that had a few cracks and holes. The rats had gnawed holes through the floors, so Dad had taken lids from pork and beans cans and nailed them over the holes. There were still always rats, mice and other creatures in the house. We always had D-Con settin' around and quite often would have that unpleasant smell of a mouse that was about ready to pop.

It was summertime and the windows were wide open. What was left of some cheap plastic curtains, were rustling in the breeze. The old man didn't like the sound; it disturbed his nappin' so he had tied the curtains in knots about the middle. The bottom ends had whipped in the wind 'til they were in shreds. All of a sudden there was a WHOP! sound on the floor. Both of us looked around, didn't see anything and dozed back off.

This strange sound went on for several days before we discovered a green tree frog in the middle of the floor eating a big juicy bug... After the frog finished the bug, he proceeded back up the curtain rod. When a bug crossed the floor, it was a frog in a swan dive. He nailed those bugs every time. So dad and I started catching big June bugs by the back porch lights to turn lose for the frog. Each time the bug was turned loose a bit farther from the frog, to improve on the distance of each dive. It was a beautiful site.

The summer passed. One day the frog left and went to wherever it is that frogs go. The next spring the frog left his fans in a disappointed state when he didn't show up. All winter we reminisced and planned on next summer

# A 'Mac' Story #7

## SKUNK BY THE TAIL

My dad liked to show off to the kids about the "hill" ways. Things like how to break a possum's neck with your bare hands so as not to put a hole in the pelt from a gunshot. The fur buyer might dock you for a hole. It didn't make much sense to the kids since a possum hide was only worth a dime, but we were eager learners.

Two of us boys caught this great big possum, one of those that was almost black.
We carried him up to the light by the tail and dad proceeded with the neck breaking demonstration.

"You put your left hand around his neck behind his head. Then slip your right hand under his lower jaw, and snap the head back over your left hand and break his neck." he bragged. "Now pay attention." He grabbed that possum behind the head with his left hand and grabbed the jaw with the right hand, except his hand was in the possums jaw, not under it.

When you see your teacher with a possum hanging on his hand and another man with pliers breaking out teeth, that's education. They ended up shooting that possum.

A year or two later it was time for another lesson. "If you grab a skunk by the tail and get his feet off the ground, he can't spray you." After the possum, doubts ran through our heads.

There was a cur dog that took to going coon hunting. Most cur dogs just sat at the house and barked, but this one liked the excitement of the hunt. Coon hounds usually just disappear into the dark and are never seen until they 'tree'. This cur dog liked to show off. You could hear his trotting around over to the side and then he would run by as fast as he could, showing off. He would trot around on the other side for a while, and then he'd pass you like his ass was on fire.

You couldn't lock the cur dog up. He would always get loose and show up. He would show up to anyone that was hunting. Sometimes he would scare the hell out of a stranger when he sprinted by.

When the hounds treed, he would try to climb the tree. That damn dog would get way back and run like hell bent for election and jump up into the tree. Sometimes he would make it to a limb, and then start working his way up the tree. A lot of times he fell out and right back up he'd go, no matter how many times he fell out.

The old cur was fun to have along for a while, but he took to skunkin'. One night my dad went hunting with us boys. He usually went about once a year. They told him about the cur and his skunkin'.

"Skunks won't spray until a dog grabs them," Dad said. Shortly, the cur barked – we knew it was a skunk. Dad made a mad dash and grabbed that skunk by the tail and hoisted it into the air. The young guys ran like hell. Dad yelled "Come here and look at this skunk". We approached slowly, like we were going to a dead body. Dad carried that skunk and explained skunkdom to us boys. Suddenly the skunk reached out and grabbed a weed with its front feet!!

We still laugh and wonder if that skunk has fallen to earth yet!

Every year from September through January, while most of the other kids were scooping the loop and hanging out at the White Grill, Mac was enjoying his passion, coon hunting. Every year, at the start of coon season, he lost a girlfriend because he hunted every night, and then after season was over he would have to start his social life again. A lot of the time he just headed out in the woods and around the creeks behind his house. Other times he would hunt with his coon hunting buddies, which were all ages, and they would hunt all over the countryside. As time went on, more and more people started moving to the country on small acreages, which made it harder to hunt big expanses of woods. Of course, the most important thing was their coon dog, which was their common bond and their pride and joy. Their attire was about as important as a prom outfit; with insulated coveralls, boots, and a hat with a real fire torch on the front. It was a carbide light of course, which had water and carbide in a little can attached to the front of their hats, and when it was lit, the fire produced an amazing amount of light. The dogs were taken to the hunting spot in a dog box in the back of a truck, and would be crazy with anticipation for the hunt. As soon as they arrived, they would kick the dogs out, and the hunt was on. It was then a waiting game, just strolling through the woods waiting for the dogs to hit a track. Once the dogs treed, you would run to them and if it was in season, shoot the coon out of the tree. This may seem cruel to some but they always saved the coon pelts and sold them to the fur buyer. At those days, a coon hide would bring two dollars which would run their old Chevy's for a week. If it was out of season, they would hold the dogs while someone would climb the tree and kick the coon out, and let it get away for a while. Once they turned the dogs loose, the hunt was on again. Actually they would go coon hunting in the off season just to enjoy listening to the dogs work the track. Mac usually had Black and Tan coon hounds. He had one great dog that someone evidently stole. The dogs would venture so far that sometimes you couldn't get them to come back when you wanted to go home. They had such great sense of smell that you could throw out something of the dog's, like his blanket, and it would go back to it and you could pick them up there the next day. Sometimes you would lose a dog when it would fight a coon in the water and the coon would drown the dog. Of course the equivalent of a medal for a dog was rips in their big old long ears. The dogs loved to jump right into the fight.

Everyone had a nickname. Mac was called Sam, and one of his friends was called Toad. Well, one cold frosty night, Toad and Mac were hunting, and Toad had brand new boots. Toad had a pretty decent couple of coon dogs and Mac had a young Black and Tan. They turned them out at the old Avola Cemetery and they ran a tract down in the bottoms, and over the countryside, and through the corn fields, and then they heard them treeing at an old empty house. They ran to the dogs and just as they got there, Toad's best coon dog was treeing at the old outhouse and proceeded to drag out the biggest old 'possum they had ever seen, and the fight was on. Of course he was so embarrassed his great dog had run a ' possum track all that way that he rushed up and grabbed his dog by the collar. The next thing he knew, the 'possum had sunk his teeth in his left foot. He fell to the ground and started flinging the 'possum, trying to kick it off, going round and round. At this point, every time Mac would tell this story, he would be laughing so hard, and would demonstrate what the scene looked like. Of course the other dogs were leaping at the 'possum. Finally the boot, with the 'possum attached, came flying off and the boot had thirteen holes in it, including a 'possum tooth. It also sliced a pretty bad cut in his foot, which they checked with the Vet the next day... country medical treatment.

If you were a novice coon hunter, and went along for a wonderful evening walking in the woods under the stars, you had better have your own light, because as soon as the dogs hit a track, those guys with those flaming hats, would take off and leave you in the dark with no idea where you were.

# A 'Mac Story' #8

## TREED CAT

There is nothing that can make a man prouder or more ashamed than his coon hound. Where we come from, there are two kinds of dogs – coon hounds and cur dogs. Maybe a bird dog would be acceptable but, most of all, coon hounds and coon hunting was one of the most important of all activities. To this day, the great dogs are all mentioned by their names, and everybody has a story about them. Everyone could tell whose dogs were running by the dogs mouths. That refers to the sound of each hound's chop (fast bark) or bawl (long bark). Some dogs bawl on a track and chop on a tree. Some chop or bawl all the way. On a cold winter night there is nothing better than to hear a good pair of hounds bawling every breath on a hot track and treeing a coon. When it's done right, it's a thing of beauty. If you are lucky, you might get to see it done right just a few times in your life.

Almost every dog, like most of the owners, has some weaknesses. Some 'skunks', some 'possums', but the worst is to tree a house cat.

There was an old bachelor who earned his living as a dog trader. He hardly ever had the same hound more than a week or two. Once in a while, he would get a good one and keep it until he needed some good money. Most times he would get to a dog sales and trade. He would always take six or seven dogs. He would tie most of them to the back bumper of the car and maybe one or two to the front bumper. When someone came along looking at dogs and asking how much, they would then ask how about the one on the front bumper? "Those ain't for sale". Of course, those were the ones he sold, and then he moved another dog to the front bumper. If he traded for a dog, most times he would take them hunting at least once, and then they would be in the trade line the next week. One night he was trying out some of these new dogs. They hit a track and ran it hot. He was really getting excited- big coon for sure. They treed, real hot, a great big tom cat on the front porch of a widow woman's house.

When you're coon hunting, most anything can happen, but he is the only man anyone ever heard of that got a wife with a poor coon hound.

# A 'Mac' Story #9

## TOOTHPICK

It was a status symbol to have a coon prick for a toothpick. The bigger the boar coon, the bigger the penis. They have a 'J' shaped one, and when dried in the sun and rubbed, it looks much like ivory. So, if you got a real big coon, it was assured that its penis would be made into a toothpick. Most people carried them on a key chain or a watch bob.

There was a woman from our town that had run off, as a girl, with a man from Wyoming, and that is where they lived. About every five or ten years, sometimes more, they would get back for a visit.

They were back, and of course, there was a big coon hunt planned. After supper these men were bragging about their hounds and one of them pulled out his toothpick and started picking his teeth. It was a big one, the biggest boar coon, by far, every treed in our parts. The old man was real proud. Of course, the boy from Wyoming saw it and made the comment.

"What's that?"

"It's a coon prick."

"I'll be damned" as he reached in his pocket and pulled out his toothpick that was probably four times larger. Now this got the old coon hunters attention. After he had some fun, the boy from Wyoming fessed up that they hunted bear out in Wyoming. They made a trade and to this day young boys marvel at the old man's toothpick.

When I was in college, most of the other students come from urban areas. One was from the east coast and had come to Missouri to get in touch with the hillbilly ways. Of course he took a likin' to me. One day he saw a big dead coon on the side of the road. He immediately thought "coon skin cap". He could go back to the east coast as Daniel Boon! So he brought the coon to me to have it skinned and made into a hat. It was summer and the coon was getting a little on the ripe side. I had to inform him that the hide would not be any good. He was really let down. Then I noticed that it was a boar coon, so I told him about the toothpick. He liked that, so we made one.

After college we went our separate ways. About ten years later we met in Chicago. We were both talking to other people when we noticed each other across the room. He grinned and reached in his pocket and started picking his teeth.

Mac enjoyed high school in Nevada, but many at the school just thought of him as a poor farm kid who would never 'go anywhere'. Little did they know, that he would become a major Midwest sculptor, admired professor with a degree from a distinguished art institute and a terminal MFA (Master of Fine Arts) from a major university, and retire with honors as a Professor Emeritus with an honorary doctorate.

While at Nevada, Mac played sousaphone in the band, and was the band president during his senior year. Of all his high school accomplishments, band and being the president, gave him a great sense of self-worth. He also played football as a guard, as did George, his old friend from the 'one room school house' days.

Mac was an average student, but his favorite class was Shop. He had a wonderful teacher, Mr. Brown. Mac felt he was the only teacher he had that really believed in him and saw his potential, and told him so, which is so important. Mac built a beautiful wooden desk in his shop class that is used to this day, and started his interest in furniture making. Of course in later years, even though his furniture pieces were functional, they were works of art.

Mac did like his art classes. His paintings were typical of high school art, but they showed he had talent. Many years later, the retired high school principal was driving through Iowa when an announcement of an important art opening of the artist, Mac Hornecker, came on the radio. The principal was so proud, he went back to Nevada and put an article in the Nevada newspaper about his experience.

At this point Mac knew he wanted to be an artist but didn't really realize his passion was going to be sculpture.

football at Nevada High School

Mac and George   Graduation    Nevada, Missouri 1962

Art class

senior picture

# TWO

## Pauline and Gordon Hornecker

Pauline was a Borghardt and grew up with one sister, Mary. When Pauline was eight, her mother died and she and her father and sister went to live with her grandparents. Children losing their mothers early in life seemed to be a common occurrence in that area, in those days.

Before her mother died, they lived about two miles from school. After they went to live with their grandparents, they were a lot closer, only one and a half miles! In those days, kids thought of an education as a wonderful gift, and would endure many inconveniences to get that education. The common story is always, "I had to walk a mile and a half to school in deep snow…." But this was the truth for Pauline and Mary. The closest distance was a mile and a half across pastures and two streams, which they made foot logs to cross. Because the one room schoolhouse only went to the eighth grade, they continued through high school at Bronaugh, Missouri. The amazing thing about that, it was a 20 minute drive from their house.

Those two girls at this young age rented a room to stay at during the week from a family in Bronaugh, and then went home on most week-ends. It was just a room, where the sisters shared a three quarter size bed, and cooked their meals on a little coal stove. Many times they would have friends stay and would all sleep in the same bed. When one girl would want to turn over she would shout "turn", and they would all turn together. Both girls started at Bronaugh at the same time and continued until they graduated from the twelfth grade. After graduation from high school the girls took the three month summer school course at the college in Springfield, Missouri, to become teachers. They taught in local one room schoolhouses, teaching eight grades for about twenty-five to thirty-five dollars a month. Pauline taught until she married Mac's dad, since it was the rule then, that teachers had to be single. After quite a few years of teaching, Mary married, moved to Alaska, and finally settled in Columbus, Ohio. She was one of the few adventurous enough to move out of 'the village'. There was so much support and friendship among all the families in the area, which were mostly related in some way, that very few at that time wanted to move away. World War II changed that, and several left the area but usually for Midwest locations like Topeka, Kansas, which was actually not too far away.

Not very much was ever mentioned about Pauline. Mac grew up not knowing much about his mother. Maybe, her history and fortitude might be where Mac got his incredible sense of hard work and steadfastness of purpose, and his unique personality that translated into great teaching skills. A mother, who has not been allowed to finish her parenting, always hopes that she will have left to her child, wonderful traits that will help him in his life.

**Gordon**, or Gord, or the 'Old Man', as he was affectionately called, was usually an easygoing, do just-what-you-have-to-do-to-get-by, happy, kept to his own business, loved to prowl around the land and area, proud watermelon grower, smart with an enormous vocabulary, eighth grade educated, and 'jack of all trades', working man.

He just loved to beat the younger 'whipper snappers' doing an algebra problem and getting the answer first by just using his common sense; or playing Scrabble and coming up with a word that everyone thought was not a word, and it always was.

Pauline and Gordon's wedding picture

*Gord was pretty quiet and never said very much but he did love to dance.*
**A Mac Story # 10**

## DANCIN' IN THE HOUSE

On Saturday night there was always a dance somewhere. People always think of a barn dance but no one in our neighborhood had a barn big enough to dance in. Most barns were just made of poles and a few sheets of tin. Anyway, most dances in the summertime were held in the dirt streets where it was hot and so dusty that sometimes the dance had to move down the street 'til the dust cleared.

A lot of times dances were held in houses. When people got there, the men would move all the furniture out into the front yard. The band usually played in the kitchen. Square dancing or just a jig was the order of the day. The kids played "hide and seek" in the darkness outside. Most people were "teetotalers" but some liked to drink, and there was always a table of food, sometimes on the front porch.

Two old buddies, that had grown up together, liked to dance. They could really cut a rug. Both were fairly short men but one was thin and the other was stocky. The little guy was feeling pretty good after a few trips out to the car.

It was time for these boys to do the dance of the night, so they got some partners. The little guy got a big fat woman and man could she dance. The stocky guy got a real tall woman (6'2" or so) that had a stiff neck so her head was tilted back. She always wore her hair back in a bun.

The band started a fast one and it wasn't long 'til everyone but these four were lined around the room clapping and stomping in time with the music. Now they were dancing and all of a sudden, the tall woman's high heel got hooked in the hammer loop of her partner's overalls. They lost their balance and broke right through the wall of the house and landed in the front yard.

The next day the two dancers, who were carpenters, fixed the house with new studs, weather boarding, <u>and plaster. That was the best thing that ever happened to that old house.</u>

Mac had always told this story, because his Dad and his buddy were the guys, and his Dad was dancing with the tall lady who got her heel caught in the hammer loop and went flying through the wall.

**Memories from Mary Ann,**

There was a lot of dancing in some old houses --- it would usually start as 'there is going to be a party tonight'...birthday party or something like that. The music was often in the kitchen...a fiddle, banjo, mandolin, and a guitar or so, and sometimes an accordion. The dance per se was usually in a bedroom. The furniture was dismantled and packed out into the yard. There was usually a jig. The next most common was square dance where all four couples just repeated the same routine, not like all the different steps put together today. One young girl was included in each square, but usually only one time per night. Everyone brought food...sandwiches, cookies, and cakes. Dad did enjoy dancing. The parties were fun and cars would park all along one side of the road.

Gord was a typical bachelor after Mac left for college. Mac was a little disgruntled when he went off to college and Gord promptly sold all the milk cows, but he did keep a few pasture cows. Of course, he grew watermelons. Gord was known far and wide for his watermelons. He always grew huge 'Black Diamonds' and 'Jubilee', and always won the blue ribbons at the yearly local town celebration, called the Old Settler's Picnic in Sheldon. He was always anxious for the Willhite Seed catalog to come so he could order some exotic watermelon to grow and have fun surprising everyone. Many years ago, he was probably the first to introduce a yellow meated watermelon to the locals. What a surprise that was!

Watermelons were a social event in Gord's life. Everyone around had to go to Gord's farm to get a watermelon. He had an old cedar tree in the front yard, with the branches cut off real high like a regular tree. Nailed on the tree was an old rusty chewing tobacco can. Every day, Gord would go to the patch, and bring up a load of big watermelons, and pile them by the tree. Now here is where the social part starts. As was the custom when you went to Gord's to buy a watermelon, you would lie around under the tree and visit for a while and eat some watermelons. Of course, you only had to eat the 'heart' of the melon and then throw the rest to the cows. Gord had a unique way of bouncing the melon on both ends and then breaking it open to show the heart just lying there, turned loose from the seeds. You would pick up that big hunk of heart and it was so juicy, as sweet as candy, and so firm. After leaving home, Mac would perform this technique to the amazement of HIS watermelon eaters. The only problem was, it ruined you for life from being able to enjoy a whole melon. After getting your fill of watermelon hearts and visiting, you then chose the watermelons you wanted to buy and put whatever amount of money you wanted in the rusty old Prince Albert can nailed to the tree. When the watermelon pile got low, whoever was around could load up and go to the patch with Gord for more melons. It was hard for kids and adults alike to pick which part of this was more fun, eating, or a trip to the patch. The family would gather there on weekends. After spending all day lying under the tree eating watermelons with people, you felt like you were going to explode. What great memories for everyone, young and old, and such a simple, stress-free experience. Gord usually mentioned that the family never seemed to be around when the patch needed to be hoed, but arrived to enjoy the harvest. But after Mac's wife, who was a city kid, hoed the watermelon seedlings and left the Morning Glories, Gord thought it might be a good thing not to have help. In later years, Mac would go to the refrigerator to cut off a big slice of watermelon and the middle would be absent....a mystery!

Next to socializing over his watermelons, Gord's next most enjoyable passion....deterring the kids from stealing his melons. He planned a different spot for his patch each year with different deterrents. One year he planted the patch just down the side road, which he could see from his bedroom window. He could hear the cars coming down the gravel road with their headlights turned off. The kids thought they were so smart. Gord would then sneak down to their car and start hitting it with a rubber hose, which sounded like he was tearing the car apart. Out of the patch the kids would come yelling "Gord, we're coming, we're coming!".

Another year, down in the barn lot, he had an old trailer made from the back of a pickup truck bed and he filled it with watermelons. When the kids tried to sneak up and steal the melons, they soon realized Gord had put an electric fence on the trailer. About the time they got a good shock, Gord would turn the yard light on by a switch he rigged up beside his bed, and they would fall all over themselves trying to get away.

Fifty years later, when those 'kids' get together, they still reminisce and tell their tales about getting into Gord's watermelon patch. It was a yearly challenge for them and a fun time for him.

Gord's watermelon money probably amounted to quite a bit. At the end of each day, during watermelon season, he would bring in the can and just dump it out on top of the dresser in his bedroom. Now, the doors to the house were always wide open in the summertime, whether he was there or not. The pile would get so high that it would spill onto the floor. The grandkids always marveled at all the change they could find under the bed. When he needed money he would just go get some from the pile. Most people would be counting their money each day, to see how much they made, but that part just didn't interest him.

Many people of that era got by on poor farming and a milk and egg check. Gord milked cows and had a small amount of livestock, but his main source of income was fixing things for other people. This would probably be called a 'jack of all trades'. He did everything, from putting a new metal roof on a barn to fixing a well pump. He never wanted to have a lot of money and did just what he had to do to make ends meet.

In his later years, at different times, he was the township tax assessor and collector. The job paid something, but not very much. At that time you would send in your own assessment to the courthouse and pay the collector directly.

Sometimes his 'jack of all trades' turned out to be working with little pigs, as explained in another one of Mac's Stories.

## A 'Mac' Story #11

# ASSHOLES

Almost everybody in those days had some chickens, hogs, and milk cows. This was a time that looked like that image you have, when you think "family farm".

Things were changing. Hybrid corn, the county agent, 4-H, FFA, artificial insemination, and selective breeding were all the talk.

Most people just had a few hogs and they were the old lard type or razor back type. There was a saying, "If you picked them up by the ears and their ass went below their snout, then they were ready to butcher." So there were a lot of people trying to upgrade and get a meat type hog.

My Uncle bought a high powered boar hog, a Landrace. They were long hogs (an extra pork chop) so more meat. Also he had bought more sows, more than he would normally have. He was in the hog business in a big way.

People came from miles around just to see this fancy hog. As soon as they could get on the list, they used this hog to breed their sows.

Now this was a busy hog. Every once in a while you could see him being driven down the road to the next farm. At first he was hard to drive, but after a few times he seemed to know what lay ahead.

The first pigs were born from Ol' Hy-Power, looked just like him, but within a few days some would start to bloat and then die. One Sunday afternoon my Uncle and Dad were looking at the pigs. It was strange how they were just dying. They caught one that didn't look too good to check out. He looked normal but there was definitely something wrong. Then they noticed that he had no anus. It looked normal but there was no hole. So as my Uncle held the pig around the middle with both hands, my Dad, with his trusty Barlow, poked a hole. That pig was like a deflating balloon. The spray was out of control with a rather powerful odor. So they caught all the pigs that were bloated and performed surgery. They all lived and grew up to look just like Ol' Hy-Power.

As expected, everybody's pigs had the same problem. So my Uncle and Dad went from farm to farm making assholes, as if there weren't enough around already.

,

Gord loved to prowl around and see things, whether it was in the woods or around the countryside. It was common for him to load up the car with friends and widow women and take them on an excursion to see something he was wondering about. He was limited in distance only because he had to be back at milking time, when he was milking, or take care of the livestock.

On one of his prowling adventures, at the age of 62, he got acquainted with his second wife, Nellie. She actually lived on the farm next to Mac's sister, Bonnie, which was several miles away. When they started dating they were like junior high kids in love. Mac and his family would drive seven hours from northwest Iowa to visit. To their surprise, as soon as they arrived, Gord would be shaving and sprucing up, and leaving them to go have dinner with Nellie. During a family potluck Gord and Nellie would get their plates and go outside and set on the steps by themselves together.

One day Mary Ann called Mac in Iowa and said she had heard Gord had gotten married, so Mac just picked up the phone and called him. Sure enough, he and Nellie had gone over the state line to Miami, Oklahoma, which was famous for quick marriages. You could get a license and a wedding, with the Justice of the Peace, in one quick trip. Who knows when he was going to tell his family.

Mac and his sisters had been noticing several major things Gord was doing, but didn't think to wonder why. Gord pushed the old house over into the garden area and burning it. He then dug and built a basement for a new house. Mac went down and helped with the framing. It was built pretty fast and was a nice two bedroom home. Of course the purpose probably was to have a nice home for his future bride.

They had a wonderful married life together although very short, but Gord was very happy. Nellie was a hard worker, great cook, all around nice person, and had a wonderful family of kids and grandkids that liked Gord. His only complaint was "she is just too darn neat and clean!" It was quite a change for him to have to take off his shoes at the door.

Gord was actually pretty clean and neat compared to some of his colorful neighbors, although these characters were what made the area so unique and interesting.

A 'Mac Story' #12

## OLD BACHELOR DAN

He was an old bachelor so there was no one to tell him what to do or how to act. His house had a narrow path on the floor between the nuts and bolts he had spread out –sometimes they were almost sorted to size. He also had stacks of peanuts which always seemed to be in motion. In the living room was a warm morning coal stove and two or three buckets of coal, an old oak and leather straight back divan, and a rocking chair. Sometimes he used the divan for a bed when it got real cold, but he did have a bed in another room which also had several gunny sacks of peanuts stacked under it, with more stacked up in the corner. Some of the peanuts were probably twenty years old but mostly there were just empty hulls and mouse droppings.

In the kitchen, he cooked on a coal stove. He had a table and a couple of chairs. On the table was an oil cloth that had seen better days, and his plate and dinnerware. The plate would always be upside down because he never washed it. He just sopped it out with a slice of bread and turned it upside down to wait for the next meal. Also there was a ridge of cow manure where he came in the back door from the barn. There was a half-moon shape where the door leveled it off each time it was opened.

His house had a unique aroma. Cow manure mixed with the smell of milk on this overalls as well as the smell of mice. In the wintertime, he would sit in the front room and spit tobacco juice on the hot stove. Not only did it smell, but it would make your eyes sting like crazy.

He always wore blue overalls and only bought one pair at a time. He milked three or four cows and would always get milk on the knees. He never washed those overalls; he just bought new ones when they cracked at the knees, about two pair a year. He had a suit that he wore to church. He never missed church so he did take a bath on Saturday night.

He never spent any money to fix anything. If it fell down, he just left it there. One time the wind blew down his chicken house. That winter the chickens started getting cold roosting in the trees, so he rolled down the window on his car so they could get in out of the weather. Needless to say, chickens left bodily functions as they roosted on the back of the front seat. He never cleaned it up; he just sat in it when he went to town. Those blue overalls turned white to brown with a soft touch of feathers on the backside. On Sunday, he would put down some layers of paper to keep his suit clean. He never took those out either, so before long his head was almost touching the ceiling.

He had a fiddle and use to play and sing for the neighborhood kids. His favorite song was "Get Away Old Maid, Get Away." Also, he liked to take us fishing and show us how to use a fish hook and some string on a hand cut willow pole. He would use a bolt nut for a sinker and a corn cob for a cork. This is when he was the happiest and sang one old song after the other.

He was full of wisdom, especially the old ways. He could keep kids mesmerized for hours. He liked candy bars and Baby Ruth was his favorite and besides kids shouldn't chew tobacco, but when he offered his peanuts from those moving sacks…that was a hard decision.

Electricity didn't come to our neighborhood until the fifties. And he was one of the last to have it put in. He was happy with coal oil lamps. He usually went to bed at dark and didn't get up 'til daylight anyway. He hired my dad and a friend to wire his house, and as the custom of those days, he asked them to stay for lunch. He would go kill a chicken. While he was out getting the chicken, Dad's friend wondered if they should eat in such filth. My Dad said, "You can always eat once what other people live on."

His life style finally caught up with the old man. He sang and milked until the day he died at nine-two." Get Away Old Maid, Get Away."

---

**Memories from Mary Ann**

Mary Ann Sprinkle and I saw Uncle Dan differently, just filthy. We had to sweep his house and wash his bedding once a year – it was black. We did enjoy playing the Victrola. He never gave us any candy but he took the neighbor boy to town with him every week and bought him a sack of candy. We would sometimes stop in on our way home from school just to check his dirty plate and play a song or two on the Victrola. Bachelor Dan's nephew's wife would have us clean his house, and on that day she would usually take a load of kids up to Slant Rock swimming. We would all be standing up in the back of an old pickup, filthy as could be and with the dust flying behind the old truck, heading down the dirt road. Work and play and bathing could all be combined.

# A 'Mac Story' # 13

## 20 YEAR OLD PEANUTS

Almost everyone shared the work, men and women, milking cows, gardening, and the like. There were however, some tasks that seemed to be done mostly by men and others mostly by women. While most of the people didn't have much, their places were kept clean and neat. Of course, there were always exceptions. For instance, most bachelors were dirty because women kept house better and seemed to care about cleanliness. For a woman to have a dirty house was unusual.

There was this old couple that never owned a house. They always rented and were usually late with that. He was real tall and she was real short. They kept everything. This house just had trails between boxes and cans and the like. He smoked Bull Durham or Prince Albert and had saved all the sacks and cans for years. They cooked on a wood cook stove in the kitchen. They were getting feeble, so a relative had bought them some coal so they didn't have to cut wood.

They had some pets. A blind dog had all the trails memorized and had no trouble getting around in the house but needed to be watched outside, or he might get lost. They also had a parakeet, which was their pride and joy, but they never did have any kids.

One time their landlord wanted to tear down the shack they called home, so they were forced to move. We all helped them move to the next house down the road. Load after load of sacks, cans, and boxes. The only furniture was a feather bed, three or four chairs, a table, the stove, and a dresser. None of it was any good. One of the chairs had been fixed with baling wire and a stick to twist the wire tight. This was not uncommon because about everybody had one or two chairs fixed that way. Anyway, we got it all moved to the new place.

The old place looked strange all emptied out. They had lived there for over twenty years. It had a smell, a mixture of Bull Durham smoke, coal and coal oil. It hadn't been wired for electricity so they used a coal oil lamp. It was sort of brown in there with the yellow light of fall shining through the dirty windows. There was a beam of light hitting right on this circle on the floor as well as a big arch of white on the wall where the bird cage had been for twenty years!

The new place was a lot bigger and had electricity. We got them all moved in about one o'clock. They were so grateful; she fixed us all lunch of mustard and sugar sandwiches and some peanuts we found when we were moving. They argued about the peanuts as to whether they were twenty or twenty-two years old.

They both lived into their eighties. The old dog never did get used to the new place. He was like a pinball machine just a bouncin' off of one thing to the next. They had several more birds but never cleaned the cage. Twenty year old peanuts may not taste the best, but they're mighty good when it's all you got.

**Memories from Mary Ann**: This is a relative who was raised by an uncle. This lady was the one that made biscuits that were so hard the dog would not even chew on them.

Like all of the Hornecker men, Gordon died too young. He had hernia surgery and complications of a twisted intestine. A few days after the second surgery for the twisted intestine and recovering well, he threw a clot in his lung and died. He was only 65 years old.

Nellie continued to live on the farm until she died about three years later. Gord had not made out a will, so half of the family farm went to Nellie, and then when she died, it went to her kids. Mary Ann ended up buying the farm, at an auction on the courthouse steps, to keep it in the family and live there after their retirement.

Shortly after Gord died while Nellie was living, a tornado went through while she was in the house, and took off the roof. She was not hurt, but the house was ruined and rebuilt with the insurance money. After Mary Ann retired, she and her husband remodeled and built on to the house. To this day, it is the favorite place for all of the kids and grandkids to visit, with cows, horses, four-wheelers with lots of places to ride, and ponds to fish. It is like Grand Central Station with all the family coming and going.

The old home place
Mac's home until he left for college, Hwy BB , Sheldon, Missouri

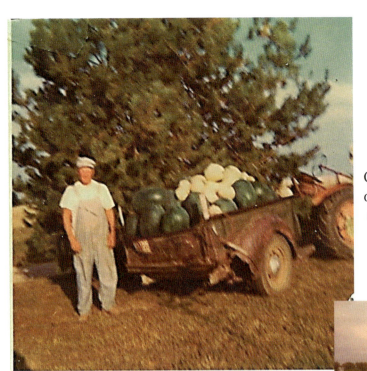

Gord, with his wagon load of melons, ready for the days' watermelon customers

Gord, in his watermelon patch

# THREE

## COLLEGE?

Joplin Junior College, Joplin, Missouri
September 1962

After Mac graduated from high school he didn't know what he was going to do. A lot of the people his age around there, went up Highway 71, about two hours to Kansas City, and worked for Hallmark Cards. Mac's dad wanted him to go into the service.

As sheer luck would have it, one day a good high school buddy and fellow football player, stopped by the farm. He was going to go to Joplin, about 60 miles away, to try out for a football scholarship at Joplin Junior College, and wondered if Mac wanted to ride along. Mac wasn't doing anything, so he jumped in the car. While he was there the coach looked at Mac and asked him if he wanted to try out too. Mac thought he might as well since he was there, though he hadn't even thought about going to college. Well he made the team and started down the path of this sculptor's amazing life.

The great thing about the football scholarship was it paid for his tuition and books, and he washed dishes in the cafeteria his first year, for free breakfast and lunch. The fabulous cooks were good old experienced farm ladies. They loved Mac because he liked everything they cooked. They made sure he ended up with a lot of extra food, like piles of pork chops and homemade rolls. He was a growing football player after all, with a bottomless stomach.

The first year at college, Mac, along with most of the other out-of-town football players, black and white, stayed at the YMCA. It was located just a couple blocks north of Joplin Junior College, They had rooms all on one floor and had a wonderful time together, always pulling pranks on each other. The rooms had with transit top windows, so if you got on someone's shoulders you could crawl through the window. They never knew what they would find in or done to their rooms. Of course 'short sheeting' and strange things in your bed were always happening, which were just a little calmer than today's antics. Soon after moving into 'the Y', Mac and his new football friends wanted to go out to eat. The black guys said they couldn't go with them. Mac said, "What do you mean you can't go with us?" When they explained to them that they weren't allowed in the restaurant because they were black, Mac and his friends said, "Heck you can't!" and away they all went to eat. No conflict ensued so they got away with it. That was Mac's first confrontation with racism. He was so naïve.

College went along pretty much as normal. The Junior College, which was referred to as JUCO, was city and county supported. It was actually pretty big with about twelve hundred students. They were mostly from the city of Joplin or the surrounding county, since they got free tuition. Most of the professors had their PhDs, so the quality of the curriculum was excellent. Mac was on the Student Council and very active and the social life was vigorous, with dances, football games, pep rallies, and parties. Everyone hung out in the cafeteria between classes. It was the social place to be and have fun. Of course, all the high school classmates, who went off to the big universities, would have thought it was pretty mediocre, but everyone got to be so well acquainted, and close to each other, including their professors.

Mac was quickly known for his art ability. Everyone would set around in the cafeteria and think of things for him to draw. "Mac, draw a horse.", "Wow!"; "Mac, draw a cow.", "Wow"; "Mac, draw a dog.", "Wow!". Of course he would whip out the drawings so fast that they were really impressed. He was the art star. Looking back, it is funny, because the first thing Mac would tell his art students, when he became a college professor was, "I don't want to see any darn dogs or cats"!!

The art teacher and Mac were good friends and had a special bond, although he was very eccentric and was mainly a poster artist. For Mac's two years at JUCO he really never had anyone give him much art direction. He just produced art on his own, although, on a pretty immature level. Being the school's art star gave him a lot of confidence. In his second year he filled the large glass case, in the main hallway, with his first art show. The show let everyone know that he had a little more depth to his art than the ability to draw animals.

While living at the 'Y', Mac worked as a lifeguard and handed out towels at the swimming pool. With the fifty cents per hour he made, he bought a twenty-five dollar savings bond every month. He always kept his first twenty-five dollar bond and said it was his 'ace in the hole'. After all these years, it is probably worth a whopping thirty-five dollars. That hole would have to be pretty small. Of course his sister, Mary Ann, sent a letter every few days with a few dollars tucked in, along with a list of words he had misspelled in the last letter he sent her.

There were always a few part time jobs for those who wanted work. Mac was always eager for ways to make some money because he was his sole support. He scooped manure at the stockyards, worked a summer for the Joplin Parks Department, and 'hustled' cokes at the Memorial Hall in Joplin. He would work most of the events at the Memorial Hall but mainly on Saturdays, the professional wrestling night. His future wife's parents had the concessions there. He would have a tray with a strap that went around his neck that held twenty-five Coke cups already iced and filled. He would make five cents for every cup he sold. He worked the most lucrative area, which was the rows right around the ring. The same people came every Saturday night- wrestling fanatics. Since Mac was a huge guy the regulars thought he fit right in and loved him. Two very old crippled ladies, walking with canes, would be at ringside every wrestling night, and always gave him a big tip. They were so dangerous to be around, because they would be flinging their canes around in the air, and trying to hit the wrestler that they didn't like.

The Promoter had the lucrative southern mid-west territory out of Tulsa, and had become good friends of Mac's girlfriend's parents. On afternoons before the matches, everyone would be in the large back room, just off the concession area and ticket booth, getting ready for the evening's event. They would always be there early along with all the wrestlers, just setting around and 'shootin' the shit'. At this point Mac was about 6 foot, 230 pounds, with a 17 ½ inch neck and arms to match. The promoter was always putting the pressure on Mac, trying to recruit him to be one of his wrestlers. Some of his wrestlers were pretty famous in the wrestling world, so it was a compliment, but little did the promoter know, Mac was not a 'fighter' type, he just looked like it.

The second year of college, Mac and three other football friends rented an upstairs apartment. The other guys had no cooking skills, so Mac became the cook, and the others had to do all the house cleaning. He knew how to eat cheap and everything was made from scratch . One night they would have spaghetti and the next night they would have fried chicken, mashed potatoes and gravy, and homemade biscuits. These were pretty much their mainstays. They never got tired of the fried chicken. Of course, back then a whole chicken would only cost less than ten cents a pound and potatoes were cheap but filling. One of the boys wrote an article in the school newspaper that is very telling about Mac's character.

**Tony Cano Pays Hornecker A Tribute**
from the 'The Chart' Joplin Junior College Newspaper 1964

"When I came to Joplin last August, I never dreamed I would soon be meeting my 'mother away from home', Mac Hornecker. The day I met Edward Mac Arthur Hornecker for the first time, I felt we would get along very well. He struck me as a man who knew nothing about cooking, ironing, and all the other essentials of housekeeping, but was I ever wrong! As soon as school started, Mac and I along with our other two roommates began our newly-acquired jobs as housekeepers.'

"We quickly sensed that Mac was to be head man; not by vote but he seems to know about cooking and everything else, which incidentally proved my previous theory wrong. Mac soon set us straight on our specific house duties, and off we went to the supermarket with 'mother'.

"I sensed a huge buying of canned goods, but again I was proven false. We arrived at the apartment loaded with spices, fresh vegetables, meat, poultry, and not one can whatsoever. Mac seemed to be able to cook as well as any woman, and till this day we have not opened a can of pork and beans. His greatest pride is his soda biscuits which won a prize for him in a cooking contest.

Being a sophomore and experienced in school work, he quickly set up study halls every night for all of us. If we even intended to omit one nightly study, he would nonchalantly say; "A football player who flunks out of school this year will do us no good next year", so we studied every night including one night out of the weekend.

"He constantly told us that we would probably have a hard time the first semester, but there were no excuses for future semesters. Now I wonder, how anyone can guide us so smoothly in everything we do, and yet not boss us around. Not many can do so, especially a man, but our 'mother away from home,' Mac Hornecker, is accomplishing such a task.

# FOUR

## MAC AND MARIE

The Football Player and the Cheerleader
Joplin Junior College, Joplin, Missouri
September 1962

It all started at a sock hop mixer dance, the first week at Joplin Junior College, where some of Marie's fellow college friends met Mac. One of the girls who lived in Joplin, on a ranch, had a really cool tack house with a big stone fireplace. The girls decided to have a party and invite all the guys they wanted to get to know better and Mac was on their list. Of course they invited very few other girls (Hum, maybe no other girls) insuring the odds were in their favor. At the party Mac and Marie started talking and got into a conversation about who could jump the highest. Marie of course thought she could, because after all, she was now a cheerleader. What a 'come on line', but it worked. They went outside by a tall fence post and had their funny 'jump off' laughing and teasing each other. They probably didn't remember who could jump the highest, but it sealed the deal, and they were a couple from that night on.

A few days later, Mac stopped her in the hall between classes and shyly asked her to go with him to Homecoming, and she accepted. A few days before Homecoming was the traditional Homecoming bonfire building night. Everyone scoured the town for wood, stopping at houses and asking for wood like they were on a 'can drive'. Of course someone always came up missing an outhouse, which was essential for the topper. What fun they had rushing back with their stash and working to make the highest pile in history. That was their first date, followed the next night by the pep rally and bonfire (date number two), followed by the next night with the football game and Homecoming dance. They doubled dated with a friend of Marie's and another football player. During the game, the other player broke some ribs, so they ended up spending a large part of the evening at the Emergency Room.  But, they didn't care about missing most of the dance. They were just smitten and so happy to be together.

The next weekend they double dated to the drive-in movie.  The name of the movie has long been forgotten but Mac had his arm around Marie and kissed her for the first time and they both actually saw fireworks.  They talked about that kiss so many times throughout their life.  They were both in shock but knew from that moment, this was forever.

Marie was a city kid from Joplin and was able to go to JUCO free because she lived in the county.  It had been a county Junior College but was just switching to become a state school, Missouri Southern College and then to Missouri Southern State University. The only cost for her first two years of college was one hundred twenty dollars for book rental. Since Mac was on a football scholarship, paying tuition, books, and fees; Mac and Maries first two years of college cost them together a grand total of the one hundred twenty dollars.

She was definitely a city kid, from a middle class family, that lived in a two bedroom bungalow.  In hindsight, it was so small by today's standards, but Marie never thought of it as small, or that anyone's house was any bigger or better. That was something special about those times. She actually didn't realize it was so small until going by to see it after the Joplin Tornado. Her grade school was Irving Scool that was on the epicenter and leveled, was just 2 blocks north of her house and eight blocks from the hospital. Her grade school, junior high school, and high school were demolished. The next year, at Marie's 50th reunion, the committee had a brick for each of them, from the dean of students wall, thinking they all had probably spent a lot of time in her office.

Mac was poor, so they always went 'dutch'. He was so suave and debonair! After a formal dance, still in formal attire, he took Marie to Griff's Hamburgers (like a poor McDonalds) for cheap hamburgers and they still went 'dutch'. Marie didn't mind at all which showed how much she cared about Mac. On the weekends, when he worked the pool at the 'Y', Marie fixed and delivered him great lunches. Her parent's grocery bill had to go up quite a bit. She would always stick in one of those huge dill pickles in its own rapper. That was a real treat.

Thanks to football and good eating, Mac was a stout, strong as an ox, 230 pound, 17.5 inch neck, hunk of a man. Through time his proportions changed, but till the day he died, he was thought of as 'strong as an ox'. At the university in Arkadelphia, where he later taught sculpture , they would say "We need five guys to lift that--- oh Mac is here, I guess we just need two guys!

Marie, knowing she was going to get a degree in Pharmacy, got a job at Freeman Hospital in Joplin during those JUCO years. The job was working in the Pharmacy after school and on week-ends for seventy-five cents per hour. She alternated the schedule with another student, and they would work in the afternoon after school, until the pharmacy closed late in the evening. Those hours included working after 5:00 pm, when the pharmacist left, and they would also be alone on the weekends. They filled all the meds for the hospital and patients. It was a lot of responsibility, but invaluable experience.

Mac had several other jobs. One day the stockyards called and wanted some guys to shovel out the pens. Mac and a friend happily took the job at two dollars and fifty cent per hour. They thought before and after that they had landed a gold mine of a job. They were both farm boys and were used to doing that job for free. Mac also worked the first summer with a fellow JUCO student, for the Joplin Parks Department, cutting and clearing brush. That was a hard job but it allowed him to stay in Joplin, instead of going back to Sheldon, so Marie and him could be together.

Mac did need to go back to Sheldon that spring to have hernia surgery. Their family doctor was a big tall loud-mouth crusty old guy with just three fingers on his right hand, but they all thought he was cool. In hindsight and for what it is worth, he was the same doctor who performed the two last surgeries on Mac's dad before he died. Marie got on a bus to go up Highway 71 to see him in the hospital in Nevada, Missouri. She had never traveled on a bus before and was so unprepared and naïve, that she got off the bus too soon at Milo, Missouri, thinking they had not stopped at Nevada. Of course Milo was a little bitty town, before you got to Nevada. Luckily a kind man drove her up the road into town to the telephone office to call for someone to pick her up. Well, as a city kid, she knew she was in another world when the telephone office was in a lady's home and the switchboard, with all the plug-in wires, was in her living room.

When Mac went to register in college they ask him for his telephone number. He told them, "two longs and a short". Of course that prompted a bewildered look. They had an old crank party line phone on the wall. Mac went home and asked his dad if they had a telephone number and his dad said they did but Mac had never known anything but 'two longs and a short'.

When Marie finally got to his hospital room, after his hernia surgery, the room was filled with his relatives. While she was there he asked her for a drink. Trying to be so attentive she jumped up and picked up the urinal thinking it was a pitcher of water. They all wondered what planet this girl came from and Mac's relatives told that story about her many times over the years.

As the first year went along, they went to the farm quite often for the weekend to see Mac's dad. He was a wonderful person, so smart for just having an eighth grade education, and so interesting. Marie, being a city kid came from an immaculate home, that was swept and picked up before they were allowed to go to bed. Going to the farm was like a breath of fresh air, with a twist of total uniqueness. You didn't worry about anything, and could wear cutoffs and a sweatshirt all weekend and just enjoy a simple life, which was so interesting.

The rectangle house of four rooms; kitchen, living room, and two bedrooms, was all connected with doors between them. A wood stove was in the living room, which heated the whole house until it would pretty much go out at night. There was no running water, but a large bucket of water was on a stand in the kitchen for drinking and water when needed. The water had so many minerals and iron in it that the bucket was crusty and black. When you made instant tea with it, you ended up with a glass of ' coal black' water. One has to remember that since Mac's mother died when he was nine months old, and after his sisters left, Mac and Gord were bachelors and lived the bachelor life for many years. Gord would bring in wood, open his arms just droping it on the floor by the stove, and the bark would go flying all over the room. When a mouse chewed a hole in the floor, Gord just nailed a Pork and Bean can lid over the hole. On the corners of the room, there would be shelves of cobwebs, and the plastic curtains that Mary Ann would put up and occasionally replace, were chewed and tattered off at the bottoms from flapping in the wind, when the windows were open.

The bathroom for the house was the two-holer outhouse, out the back door. One would guess a two-holer was a cut above a one holler. This one was a real special experience since it leaned backward at about a twenty degree angle. You thought at any moment in the middle of your job the whole thing was going to tip over with you inside. Of course there were other exciting things about Marie's new found experiences with the outhouse; like the fact that your job just dropped down to the ground, forming a growing hill that would get closer and closer to your behind. Well, the solution to that problem was to lean a little to one side to get a few more inches of use from that hole . When that technique was exhausted, you had to move to the other hole; hence the luxury of having a two-holer!   Of course the luxury was short-lived when the second hole developed the same problem. When that happened, Gord would have to shovel it out. The outhouse also had two boards missing in the back, right behind the seat, were everyone could see your 'behind' if they were coming down the road. Also a little board was missing on the front by the floor, that was just big enough to let in the little dogs or cats.  In the dark of night the animals loved to run in through the hole when you were in there, scaring you to death. Needless to say you learned to 'hold it' until morning, if you possibly could.

The first time Marie went home with Mac to the farm for the weekend, Gord and Mac slept together in one bedroom and she slept in the other.  Not only did Mac and his Dad have each other for warmth, but they had an electric blanket, and Marie had just a pile of blankets.  She was trying so hard to be a really good sport and not a spoiled city kid, but she was so cold she wore all her clothes, her sweatshirt with the hood on, and gloves. When she woke up in the morning, she had snow on her bed that had come in through the cracks in the walls!!  The visit after they were married, Marie crawled into bed but felt something by her feet.  She pulled the covers back to find a dried up dead mouse that had probably ate D'con and crawled up there to die. Needless to say, after that she always checked all the covers before going to bed.

When Mac and Marie would arrive the phones would start cranking, calling all the relatives.  Then there would usually be an impromptu wiener roast at a huge brush pile Gord had made somewhere on the farm. Relatives came from all directions with food, and a great time would be had by all.

On Sundays they would all gather at one of the aunt and uncle's houses. Marie's first Sunday get-togethers with Mac's family was at his Aunt Helen's.  Now Marie had been raised on a dinner of a meat, a potato, and a vegetable (alternating each meal from a choice of about four common vegetables), and a dessert.  Well, when this family got together, the table would start out with the appropriate number of bowls and then like magic the food started coming out of the freezer, oven, just everywhere, until there would be thirty dishes on the table.  All kinds of vegetables she didn't know existed, homemade noodles, homemade pies, meats, and 'mashed taters' and gravy appeared.  It was always a wonderful feast.  Then after everyone ate, they would all sit down circling the living room in all the chairs and lying on the floor, and proceed to fall asleep.  Being a proper city girl, she didn't know what to do so she just sat there quietly, being the only one awake, just looking around the room at these snoring people, waiting for them to slowly, one by one, wake up.

When the weather was nice, they were always out prowling in the woods hunting for pawpaws; or going to 'caves', which were actually just small cut outs in the rock ledges above the streams; hunting  for Morel mushrooms; and  just exploring.  New ones on the scene, and especially city kids, always had to be tested. One of Marie's first hikes was to show her pawpaws, which was pretty cool.  On the way, Gord wanted her to taste the root of the Jack-In-The-Pulpit.  Well she chewed a little bit and her mouth and throat started burning so bad she couldn't stand to open her mouth, because even the air made it worse.  She wanted to be such a good sport that she just smiled, with her eyes watering down her face.  Then Gord thought she should try chewing some Slippery Elm Bark. Well, when you chew it, it gets larger and larger until your mouth is full of a huge bunch of mush, which is actually pretty funny.  Marie guessed everyone had to take their turn at these interesting wrinkles of nature, and she guessed she passed the test.  When they finally got to a cave,

Gord asked her if she had ever seen a Doodle Bug. Of course she hadn't, so he dropped to the ground on all fours with his mouth just barely above the sandy floor and started yelling "doodle, doodle, doodle, doodle." Well she never saw a bug of any kind come out of the sand, and to this day doesn't know if he was just pulling a city kid's leg.

It was so obvious where Mac got his love of the terrain, and became so keenly aware of all the details of the landscape and landforms around him. There are those that just see a tree or a rock, and then there are those, like Mac, who don't even realize it, but see every detail and all of the nuances. Gord not only gave Mac his mechanical skills, but instilled in him the appreciation of the land. Little did either one of them have any idea to what extent those skills would be used, or that any of those skills were being passed on from father to son. It just happened.

Mac brought his own car to college. It was a '49 Ford, light blue with a black side door. He had put a telephone in the glove compartment, which Marie thought was so funny and cool. Of course it wasn't hooked up to anything, but he would occasionally open up the glove compartment and answer the phone as if someone had called. Humor was so simple in those days! Marie lived at home about 20 blocks away from school and the Y where Mac lived, so it was so convenient for him to have transportation. Unfortunately, one weekend Mac went home and a drunken lady came over a hill and hit him, totaling the car. Luckily, he did not get hurt except for breaking the bottom of his front tooth. From then on they were hoofin' it except when Mac would bring his dad's car from home – a 'titty pink' Ford coupe. Now they were talking cool!

Marie was the product of divorce parents and huge custody battles. She lived during the school year in Joplin with her dad and stepmother, and spent all of her summers in Lansing, Michigan with her mother and stepfather, whom she adored. She experienced wonderful summers with many relatives, on a block of twenty-two kids, and had fun traveling and camping. She went to Michigan until her first summer of college, when she started working at Freeman Hospital in Joplin. Her stepfather at the age of 40, unexpectedly died of a heart attack when Marie was a junior in high school. The week she graduated from high school her mother discovered she had breast cancer. They did radical surgery on her mother, but at that time there was not much they could do for breast cancer. A year later her mother noticed "a hitch in her get along" which turned out to be tumors on her spine and had metastasized to many places. She died at the age of 40, and just a few months before Mac and Marie were married.

Marie tried to keep up with her classes, with the help of some wonderful professors at JUCO and family relatives in Michigan, while she traveled back and forth to be with her mother. Marie and her mother's biggest worry was Marie's younger half-sister who was in the seventh grade. Because her mother knew it was just a matter of time, she and Marie made arrangements for her sister's care, upbringing, and trust arrangement, which in hindsight were not very good choices. Her mother's illness and death consumed a large part of their second year of college and became a sad time of their lives.

During that second year they needed to improve their GPAs. The first year was so much fun, and something they never regretted, but their grades suffered, They spent the rest of their college trying to increase those GPAs. With their futures now on a family course, and the early death of Marie's mother and stepfather and Mac's mother; Mac and Marie got serious and matured a lot. They started facing life with the thought that it can be very short, and you can't waste time or put anything off.  So graduate from college, have your children, get your careers going, visit and travel everywhere you want to see and do, and don't keep making excuses . 'Just make it happen' was their guide through life starting at a very young age. A few years later a close friend added to their life's motto, "Build Memories!".

They started working as much as possible and trying to save money. They kept asking everyone, "How much money do you need before you have enough to get married?" How silly that sounds now but they started out with seven hundred dollars to their name and had no idea how far that would take them. They were already in the "can't put anything off" mode. And don't forget, they still had that twenty-five dollar 'ace in the hole' savings bond!

Marie decided to major in Pharmacy by her junior year in high school, and had decided on University of Missouri at Kansas City.

Mac thought he could easily get a job at Hallmark Cards in the art department. When he went to talk to them, they looked at his portfolio and said his art wasn't what they wanted and to go home and draw up another portfolio in their style. Well, he did that a couple of times and never could make himself into a Hallmark artist.

Before the wedding they went to Kansas City to rent an apartment, not knowing anything about the town. They visited his cousin and rented a one bedroom, third floor walkup just around the corner. It was very old with a little galley kitchen, bathroom with a big claw footed tub, bedroom like a sun porch, and a Murphy bed that slid into a mirrored book shelf and under a raised closet. Actually it was a pretty neat apartment in its day.  Mac and Marie were just about the only ones that lived in the building that didn't have white hair, so they became the kids that they all looked after. There was one spooky girl that lived across the hall, but she always darted into her apartment like she was scared to death.

They got married on the day after finals of their second year at JUCO. Marie was nineteen and Mac had just turned twenty-one. Marie had a matron of honor and Mac had a best man and two ushers. There actually were quite a few people in the church, but it was a very cheap wedding. One of Mac's college mates sang and the church organist played the music. Marie had gone to look for a wedding dress and spotted, she thought, a beautiful light blue knee length lace dress, and so, she decided to wear what she wanted and not worry about tradition.  Of course everyone gasped when she started down the aisle in something but white, but it was the start of her life with a non-traditional artist. Marie's stepmother made the dress for the matron of honor and Marie's dad took Mac downtown and helped him pick out probably his first black suit. When Mac walked to the church in his new wedding suit, a dog chased him all the way down the street and tried to bite him.

After the wedding, a reception was held at a party room at the Holiday Inn with cake, nuts, and punch, and most people stayed a long time, and everyone had a good time. The whole wedding, including the minister, singer, organist, flowers, reception, and clothes, cost her parents two hundred dollars.

Everything was so much cheaper then, but they loved their wedding as much as their friend's weddings that cost several thousands of dollars. Mac and Marie knew they were students with a long way to go, and that they would need to be frugal. It started with the wedding, of which they always had wonderful fond memories.

They pulled out of the reception to cheering in the 'titty pink' Ford. They honeymooned at Rockaway Beach, in a little cabin near Branson. Marie fixed her first meal of pork chops and Jell-O. Mac, being the experienced bachelor, was the cook of the family and ended up teaching Marie how to cook. Actually he was quite a prize because he knew how to do everything.

Of course at that time, Branson was just a sleepy little town. They went to Silver Dollar City, which then consisted of a pottery shop, leather shop, and Marvel cave, which they had been to many times growing up. In future years a dam would be built to make Lake Taneycomo and they would take the water off the bottom of Table Rock Lake, which was ice cold. Now the famous Rockaway Beach is just for fisherman, especially those fishing for trout.

# FIVE

## Kansas City and the Kansas City Art Institute

### Kansas City, Missouri
### June 1964

Mac and Marie settled into their apartment in a convenient neighborhood not too far from the Plaza area and the University of Missouri at Kansas City, although not in walking distance. The first summer they both got jobs working downtown. Marie worked for Massachusetts Mutual Life Insurance that summer until pharmacy school started, and Mac got a full time job working for Ronson, repairing cigarette lighters. Back in those days, before the disposable lighters like Bic were invented, people paid hundreds of dollars for cigarette lighters. Since so many people smoked, the cigarette lighter was like a piece of jewelry to carry in their purse or pocket, and people had expensive lighters for their homes to put on their coffee tables. Lighters came in beautiful shapes and sizes and even made out of real gold. Mac worked full time at this job, and during the summer, bartended at night at an underground hippy coffee shop. One can't say that either job did much for his art career, but they were unique experiences.

Kansas City was an exciting place to live, even if you were young and poor. There was so much life and excitement, and so many things to do that were free. Of course, in those days, life was a lot less complicated and people would be entertained and impressed with simple things.

One day, Marie was riding the bus home from downtown and noticed a person on the bus that she had met before. It was the wife of Mac's second cousin and she was a schoolmate of Mac's from Nevada. They talked and decided to get together. It is a small world, and as it turned out they were newly married and lived in an apartment just a few blocks away from Mac and Marie. From that first evening, until the present they are very close friends. They also had another couple who went to school with Mac that had married and moved to Kansas City, and worked at Hallmark Cards. As was the case for so many that grew up around Mac, they left the area and migrated to Kansas City, got a job at Hallmark Cards, and worked there until they retired.

The three couples started getting together, at least once a week for supper, that they usually made together. After supper they would happily be entertained by playing cards or games like Badminton. It was such a fun time because they all were newly married and didn't have very much money, but they enjoyed so many activities that didn't cost anything. One of their favorite meals was tacos. They would fry the shells and fix a dozen each and eat them all, which thinking back seems amazing. Their hors d'oeuvres or 'hordy dovers', as Mac would call them, and drinks for the evening would be popcorn and Kool-Aid or lemonade. Once in a while the guys would spring for a six-pack of beer, which was a real treat. Some nights they would spend the evening and go to a large new type of place, much like a precursor to Wal-Mart. One such place was called 'Wild Woody's'. It was the kind of place that people would buy a pair of shoes and put them on in the parking lot, and just leave the old ones lying there, or buy oil for their car and change it in the parking lot and leave the cans. In other words this was a real classy place! The three couples would spend the whole evening just walking around looking at all the 'stuff' and maybe end up buying a bottle opener for fifteen cents. There was furniture in the back corner of the store. The kind of furniture that had gold tape around the rungs of a table to simulate metal inserts. They would all go back and look at the furniture and dream of the day they could afford to have furniture like that.

Some weekends they would go camping in an old canvas tent and fish. One fishing trip was to Osceola, Missouri, to fish for Spoonbill below the big dam. Spoonbill are good tasting boneless fish that weigh up to forty pounds or more and you 'snag' them. You need a big fishing rig and very large hooks. You throw out the line and pull it in with jerks and hope the hook snags a fish. If you are lucky to snag one, then the fight is on. That day they only had one large rig, so the guys took turns. That was good because it was such hard work, they each needed a break. In the afternoon the girls left with the car to get some water and snacks and on the way back stopped by a nice clear stream to play in for a while. When they got back, the guys were excited but exhausted, and a, "Where have you been!". They had hooked a Spoonbill and it took all 3 of them pulling on each other by their arms and legs to get and the fish in and them up the bank.

On another camping and canoeing trip, they were paddling down one of the many wonderful Missouri canoeing rivers and spied a cave up on a large incline from the river. They decided to stop and explore the cave. It was solid poison ivy up the incline, so one of the girls didn't go, but the rest bragged that poison ivy didn't bother them. Well since they were all in skimpy bathing suits, a few days later the girls were covered from head to toe with poison ivy rash.

Making homemade ice cream was another cheap activity these friends did often. S&H Green Stamps were all the rage back then and you would get so many stamps based on how much money you spent in participating store. You would rush home and paste the stamps into special books, and then you could get things that would cost so many books. It was like a buying bonus, but everyone was in a stamp saving frenzy and didn't think of all the time they were spending 'lickin' and stickin'. One of the best outcomes of the stamp saving adventure for Mac and Marie was for the amount of one and a forth books of stamps. They got a Half Gallon Ice Cream Freezer. It was a honey, with cheap metal gears and turning handle and a Paper Mache ice bucket. But if one would get a dollar for every half gallon of 'Tutty Fruity' ice cream that freezer made, they would be rich. It was amazing. 'Tutty Fruity' ice cream was Mac's specialty and everyone's favorite. They always used 'Junket' or rennet tablets, which when dissolved in a little warm water and added to plain milk would clabber the milk and make it thicker, like cream. It was a very cheap way to make great homemade ice cream. With enough milk to make a gallon, you would add the pulp and juice from three oranges, three lemons, three bananas, and add three cups of sugar. It was always a winner and that little freezer would freeze a half gallon in no time.

When September came along Marie started pharmacy school at the former University of Kansas City which became the University of Missouri at Kansas City the next year. At that time, there were thirty-five students in her third year Pharmacy class with only five girls in the whole program; four girls in her class and one fifth year student. The other girls went on to become an Internist, Financial Medical consultant, and MS in Nutrition, and researcher, and the fifth year student died during a pregnancy a few years after graduating. Marie was the only one who continued to practice pharmacy. In those days, no one thought of pharmacy as a career for a girl. One professor thought they were wasting their time with the girls because they were just going to get married and not work! It took years before people would not ask to see the pharmacist when Marie would step up to help them.

Marie, because of her experience working for the hospital in Joplin, got one of the plum student pharmacy jobs at Research Hospital, which was a beautiful large private hospital. She worked there about thirty-two hours a week and then full time in the summers. They always hired two pharmacy students. At night, again, the pharmacists would leave at 5:00 pm and then the two students, alternating nights, would 'hold down' the pharmacy and fill all the orders until 10:00pm. The orders would be sent to the Pharmacy by a pneumatic tube system, and the filled prescriptions would be sent up to the floors in a large container conveyor belt system. Once again the pharmacy was being operated by a pharmacy student without any oversight. It was allowed through a loophole in the law, because a doctor was on duty 24/7 in the hospital and would be 'in charge'. Of course Research was a 650 bed hospital, so that doctor could have cared less or had time to think of the pharmacy. Research Hospital was the hospital of choice of former President Harry Truman and two nights, while Marie was on duty, he was admitted. He always had a secure room at the end of the OB department. Little did they know that a lowly pharmacy student was filling all his medication orders and sending them up to be administered, without anyone in pharmacy checking her work. Marie worked at Research Hospital the final three years of pharmacy school and then as a full time pharmacist after she graduated and passed the 'boards'. She had already met her one year internship requirements, so took the boards right away and immediately started receiving full pharmacy pay which helped their finances.

The first year Mac lived in Kansas City, he took night courses at the University and worked during the daytime. He took a history course and English II. At the Junior College he had passed English I and English III but made a D in English II, which would not transfer. English was definitely his nemesis. Marie tried to convince him to check out the Kansas City Art Institute, but he didn't think he had a chance of being accepted there. So, one day when Mac was at work, Marie took his portfolio to the Art Institute and met with the Academic Dean. He was very impressed and told her he wanted to talk to Mac. They met with Mac and reviewed his portfolio, and wanted him to start the next semester. The rest is history.

The next year, Mac started at the Art Institute as a freshman art student because none of his previous art classes would transfer, along with English II, which he again received a D, from the night class at the university. Thinking back, there should have been a celebration party when he finally passed that course.

The Art Institute had a wonderful curriculum of a half day Foundations Class for first year students. The class was very large consisting of all the beginning students, and was held in a large metal 'butler building'. When grades were handed out after the first semester there were no ' A's and only four 'B's. Mac was one of those ' B's. At that moment, he knew he had a special talent and that gave him the confidence in his ability that lasted his whole life. As an artist, you must have enormous confidence in yourself, because at times you are the only one.

The most important thing that happened to Mac was tooking a sculpture class from Dale Eldred. Dale was a big 'Fin' with blond curly hair, big in stature (a former University of Michigan football player), just bigger than life, and was affectionately referred to as 'Papa Bear'. He was one to leave notes around the studio to students like "Where in the Hell have you been". Mac had always liked that one. When Mac first stated teaching, he left a big note on the door of the building that contained the art department along with education and social studies. It said, "<u>name</u> where have you been, since you haven't been in class?" Mac walked up one day to the very straight-laced, conservative Dean of Faculty who was reading the note. Boy, he thought, " I am in trouble", when the Dean very matter of fact and pompously said "I imagine this is quite effective." Dale taught Mac how to be a great sculptor and a stern but effective teacher, with no 'bull shit', and never give a positive compliment unless you really meant it.

Dale was an internationally acclaimed sculptor, renowned for large-scale sculpture that sometimes covered a block, and in his later years his sculptures emphasized both natural and generated light.

Dale had a rough, no nonsense personality that Mac enjoyed. Dale had Mac help him many times with his work, as Mac did with his students, and they became lifelong friends. He was definitely Mac's mentor. It took several years for Mac's art to not have the Eldred influence, and become his own. Mac never thought of Sculpture in small terms again. Dale instilled in Mac the love of casting, welding, grinding, and size that required the use of cranes, all of which dominated Mac's work through his later professional life.  As a professor, Mac was also thought of as super strong, big in stature, bigger than life, and intimidating – just another 'Papa Bear'.

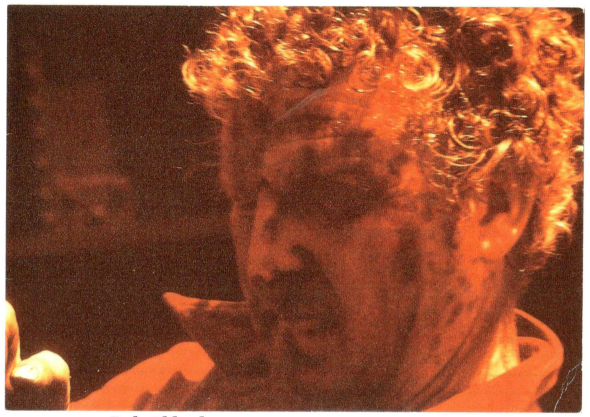

**Dale Eldred     1933-1993**     photo credit – unknown

    Dale died in an accident during the '500 year' Kansas City flood of 1993. He had, as one of his studios, an old electrical plant which had once contained large turbines. He and friends were moving the contents to a higher level when he accidentally backed up to the opening in the floor for one of the turbines, and fell to his death. He was sixty years old and had taught at the Art Institute for thirty-three years. What a tremendous loss at so young an age. Hopefully now, Mac and Dale are making sculpture 'up there' together.

    Mac was fortunate to have studied under many other wonderful professors at the Institute, such as the famous potter, Ken Ferguson. Ken was considered one of the top ceramicists in the country. He was a crusty old guy with a no-nonsense personality, which again Mac loved. After you would proudly turn a beautiful pot on the wheel, Ferguson would come along, not being nearly so impressed, and run a wire through it to show you all the imperfections or bust open a coveted finished pot. He was intimidating and after a while you got used to him being very frank. He taught Mac that being a potter didn't mean just making ordinary functional pottery, but being an artist making a piece of art of museum quality.

Mac loved ceramics. He could throw all the functional pottery, but loved the more gutsy style with a Raku glaze. It fit his personality, and there was something thrilling about pulling a piece of pottery out of a fiery kiln, and throwing it into a barrel of old leaves or other matter, and being surprised with the finished glaze.

Mac also had great classes taught by well know printmakers, like Jack Lemon, another professor at the Art Institute. Mac really enjoyed all types of printmaking, but he soon found out that he didn't want to waste time that could be used to make sculpture. But, all the skills he learned, came in handy when he taught printmaking later in his teaching career.

Jim Leedy, was another favorite teacher and friend of Mac's. He was a dynamic force at the Kansas City Art Institute for over forty years. He was quite the individual and pushed the boundaries of the students. Leedy's work encompassed all media. He mixed painting with sculpture, and pottery to clay sculpture, among many other media. He also had a crusty personality that of course Mac enjoyed. At Buena Vista University were Mac later taught, the student art organization tried to take an art trip every year. They would usually alternate between Chicago and Kansas City . Of course Mac would make the Art Institute one of the major stops on the Kansas City trip and usually he would connect with Jim, who would entertain the students in his studio. That was always a highlight of the trip.

Mac had the luck of being at the Art Institute at a time with a great bunch of sculpture students, and remained friends with many of them. Many have continued to be working sculptors, and have become important in the art world.

Most went on to get an MFA's in Sculpture and taught in universities in and out of the country, and produce acclaimed art. One went on to Chicago and worked with the famous Richard Hunt. Another became a well-known sculptor and printmaker who received his MFA at the University of California at Davis and has sculptures in major museums around the world. When this student went to the Art Institute he was remembered as having longer black unkempt hair, sloppy cloths as most art students, and bells around his ankles. He married a sculptor who is famous for her stick bronze horses, which are also in major museums all over the world. Years later he visited Mac and Marie, and Marie was taken aback by this good looking man that walked in, with his snappy Hawaiian shirt and khakis and beautifully styled white hair. It was a great reminiscing reunion and visit.

In 1993, a memorial celebration for Dale Eldred was held at the Art Institute and most of Mac's sculpture bunch came back. It was a time for sadness, but also celebration of Dale, and a wonderful time of nostalgia and storytelling. A sad footnote at this time is that in this picture , six of the ten students, of this group that returned for Dale's memorial, are now gone and hopefully also working in that studio with Dale.

Old friends and former sculpture students of Dale Eldred's at the Kansas City Art Institute
Gathering after the Memorial and Celebration service for Dale
Top: Paul Slepak, Carl Ponca, Jim Leedy (faculty), John Buck, Moose Kimball, Steve Parzybok
Kneeling: Hugh Merrill, David Coddaire, John Fernie, Mac, and Dick Hollander

    Mac had several jobs while an art student. All three years he had working assistantships to help pay for his tuition. The first year, he was a janitor and mainly swept out the large foundation studio. The next two years he had a plum assignment. He manned the desk in the library. It was usually pretty quiet in the evening until closing, so Mac would spend the time devouring all the art books. It was an especially rewarding place to spend long hours, because of the art books Mac had access to, were not allowed to be checked out of the library. He found a new hunger for art books, periodicals, and art libraries. When he taught he sent the students to the library for projects that made them search the art section in ways that they would not have done on their own. His term papers were comparison papers between two artists, whose names he would have them pick out of a hat. That required a lot of research and thinking that could not be found already written anywhere. If a student was having trouble with a direction of his art, Mac would send them over to the library with a list of books to look at, or tell them to study a certain artist for style and technique. Many times it would be like a light bulb being turned on. Until the day he died, wherever he taught, Mac would be turning in a list of art books for the library to buy and have available to the students. His most pleasurable time was to spend an afternoon in the library going through, again and again, their collection of art books and art magazines.

His second year, he got a part time job at a custom wrought iron fence company as a fence designer. Of course when he wasn't busy, he was back in the metal shop with the guys that were working with the forges and making the fences he designed, or out in the field helping to install the ornate fences.

Another job which only helped his cooking success at home was being the kitchen boss at a large fun house pizza parlor, called Shakey's Pizza. Every night people would order a pizza and never pick it up, so at closing time around midnight, Mac would come home with pizzas that had laid on top of the oven to keep warm. Mac and Marie had a big Black and Tan coonhound that waited at the door drooling in anticipation of the left over pizza. Needless to say they also provided many nights of a late supper. The job was not so bad except on nights when the crew would get the place and kitchen all cleaned up, and a bus full of army men would arrive just at closing, and all order a different pizza.

This was a very historic time in Kansas City, in 1968, and became one of 37 cities that endured riots after the assassination of Martin Luther King. The trouble started when students marched in protest because the city did not call school off for Dr. King's funeral, and the police used tear gas on the students. There were snipers shooting off buildings downtown, armed soldiers on corners with guns drawn, and curfews. A total of five people lost their lives and many were injured. A lot of threats were floating around. One of the pharmacy techs that Marie worked with, and which happened to be black, lived close to Marie's neighborhood. She had worked in the pharmacy for years and was very credible. She said there had been people contacting the black population in the area with instructions to hang a black shirt on their door, so if a riot pursued, their house would be safe. It was a scary time that lasted about a week. One night, Mac and Marie went to the apartment of a fellow Art Institute student for dinner and to play cards. During the evening army tanks were patrolling up and down the neighborhood streets. The sound of the tanks was loud, scary, and the vibration shook the whole apartment.

When Mac and Marie moved from the apartment to a rental house their second year, it just wasn't complete without a dog. Of course they had to have a Black and Tan coonhound. Snoopy was his name and was a wonderful kind dog, and became their token kid. Mac would coon hunt with a 'relative of a relative' who had expensive high powered dogs. This fellow was serious and sometimes would hunt until midnight. Snoopy had a beautiful 'mouth' but never made Mac very proud. Mac complained that he was a spoiled house dog, so was ruined as a hunting dog. Sometimes the dogs would be way off when it was time to go home. Mac would just lay Snoopy's rug down on the ground and he would smell his way back and stay with his rug until Mac would go pick him up the next day.

During Mac's last year at the Art Institute, Marie worked full time at Research Hospital. They, like all their friends, had decided to start a family and after two miscarriages, had their first child, Med Allen Hornecker. He was born three weeks late, which they allowed back then, but finally Med decided to arrive the week after Mac graduated from the Art Institute. Now living in a real house, with college degrees, going to graduate school, and a wonderful new bouncing baby boy; life was wonderful. Now they were off for the next phase in their life,

**These pictures had been selected by Mac for a future retrospective.**

Works done while at the Kansas City Art Institute

    This entire piece was cut out with an ax. Mac really liked the piece, but after a long time in this location on campus, one day Dale Eldred said in his blunt manner "Get this shit out of here". Needless to say Mac was a little disheartened – but in later years Mac's students were crying on his daughter's shoulders ( who was an art student) " Do you know what your dad said about my sculpture?...."

Laminated wood is starting to appear in Mac's work

Mac made a piece of laminated wood in this curved style for Marie's parents to set on top of their stereo. Marie's dad, after studying it for a long time, and probably wanting his daughter to be married to someone financially successful and not an artist, said, "Mac if you would make a whole bunch of these and call them *"The Circle Of Life"*, you could make a lot of money."

Walnut and Pine laminated wood sculpture in front of building on Kansas City Art Institute Campus. Did Mac notice the boots hanging from the sculpture when he took this slide? He probably did.

# SIX

## UNIVERSITY OF OKLAHOMA and MAC'S MFA

## Norman, Oklahoma 1968

As Mac was getting close to graduating from the Art Institute, he started thinking about what to do next. It sounds funny, but through the years at the Art Institute, most of the students just thought about making art. Several of the others were thinking about getting into graduate school and getting an MFA (Master of Fine Art) which is a terminal degree, and possibly teaching at the college level. One friend had applied at the University of Oregon, and one applied at the University of Oklahoma. Oklahoma sounded like a good place, so Mac applied and was accepted. Mac always had a pretty trusting and lackadaisical attitude and he really didn't do much to check into the graduate program he was applying to. Now, that sounds so strange, but maybe it was a sign of the times or part of the attitude of his upbringing.

The month before they were leaving for the University of Oklahoma, Marie was working one evening while Mac was home taking care of their son, Med. Med had gotten his first round of shots that day and was fussy and crying for the first time in three months. Mac called Marie at work, kind of worried, so when she closed the pharmacy she hurried home and parked the car, for the first time, on the street in front of their house. The next day she went to the front to get into the car, but it wasn't there. She went to the back to the garage...no car.. then to the front..and finally realized it had been stolen. They had resently bought a used sporty Chevy coupe, black and white with red leather interior...really cool. They had a used transmission installed, so the car was in tip top shape. Mac had noticed that the used transmission sure looked like a new one. The police thought it was probably an inside job and the car was stolen for that new transmission. Of course to save money, they didn't have theft insurance, so it was a total loss. Marie's parents came to the rescue and floated the money to buy a simple new Chevy station wagon, which served them well for many years.

They went to Norman in July to look for housing and rented a nice three bedroom brick home, just a few blocks from campus, from a female realtor. She spotted Mac as a 'do anything' kind of guy and through the years, paid him to fix and repair so much on their house that it really increased in value, which was the case of every house they lived in. The realtor also hired Mac to do a lot of odd jobs on her other rental houses. It was a great relationship and income source. So when August rolled around, they were off to Oklahoma and the land of the Sooners.

When Mac arrived, because another student had decided to go to a different graduate school, Mac was granted the available teaching assistantship to teach a freshman class. At that time, the teaching assistantships paid a quarter of a full-time salary. In hindsight, it was an enormous stroke of luck to have picked the University of Oklahoma. It turned out to be the primo years of their sculpture graduate program. It was a very loose program with a bunch of graduate students that had amazing comradery and work ethics that brought out the best in all of them.

The University acquired the old Air Force base which consisted of a North Base and a South Base. The South Base was mostly barracks that were used for married student housing. The North Base housed the airport, buildings that were used by NOAA for their national forecasting and storm prediction centers, and the University High School. But, best of all were several two story barracks, in which one infamous one was called '7J', the home of the art students graduate studios. There was so much good art created inside and on the vast flat grassy area outside. The studios were partitioned off on each side, equiped as each student saw fit, but open to a walkway down the middle. This allowed for interplay and friendship between the students that was so instrumental to this positive experience. Many of Mac's close friends to this day are those fellow graduate students from those days at '7J'. They scattered to all parts of the country, but have stayed in contact and have wonderful get-togethers.

One of the great advantages of the university that the sculpture students discovered, was the university's salvage yard, or University Surplus. It was a treasure trove of everything the University had replaced, broken, or discarded. It was a sea of free sculpture supplies. The pieces that were made were a little of the 'found art' kind, but many were made of materials, especially metals, that the students would have had to buy. The salvage yard made it affordable to make very large pieces.

Not only was there a closeness between the students in the graduate program, but most of them were married, and the couples became good friends. They would get together usually about once a week and pool their food, grill, and play cards. They played a lot of Pitch, but the most fun was a game called 'Nertz". It was actually double solitaire with teams of two people. Everyone played on the aces that were laid in the middle. Of course, it was always a race to the middle to place the next card and many a deck had finger tears from previous vicious competitions. The 'in' meal at the time was Fondue with Sangria to drink, made from scratch with cheap red wine. That kind of meal was great because it took quite a while to cook your food a few bites at a time, and the lengthen time promoted a lot of fun conversations.

Mac and Marie lived about eight blocks away from the OU stadium. On game day the town turned red, and the interstate into Norman became a trail of red for 30 miles. The normal attire was red cowboy boots, hat, and blazer. The graduate students could get tickets pretty cheap, but they were in the end zone. The first year, Mac and Marie did not have tickets, but could be working in the yard and hear the roar of the crowd and run in and see the touchdown on the TV, which had a little delay. The second year was the famous year of the Heisman trophy winner, Steve Owens. Mac and Marie had their end zone seats but couldn't tell what was happening unless Steve Owens ran sideways. It was really hard to watch the game with all the huge coolers around the stands, and a rather large party going on at each cooler. It was a great people watching event with all the excitement of a big college football game.

This was also the time football players received every perk imaginable. At that time, players lived in their own football dorm, and Mac walked behind it on his way home from classes. He was always appalled at the food they were served, and all that was thrown out, especially the steaks.

Joe Hobbs was the dean of the art department, and he and his wife remained good friends of Mac and Marie's. He said those few years had the best graduate students of his 44 year career of being an art department dean. Of course Joe had a large part in making it the place it was. He was very low key, but had good connections and gave the students many advantages. Joe and his wife owned a large piece of land out in the country, which was just red sand, a little hilly, with scrubby trees and an old house. It turned into the place for so many graduate school art parties. It sounds trivial, but so many art vibes and great ideas flow around when art students get together, get to know each other well, and share their art.

Some nights the film makers would put a screen up outside and all would experience their latest film projects. Sometimes sculptures would be installed around the landscape for a show. One of the most important times was when Joe put together a show with the famous sculptor, Robert Morris. He and some of the graduate sculpture students put works around the landscape and called it "Robert Morris and His Oklahoma Friends". It was an official show with a catalog. It was a great experience and looked very impressive on those future résumés.

Oklahoma City was just 18 miles from Norman and had a pretty active art community. The Oklahoma Art Council was there, along with a wonderful contemporary art gallery called the CAF (Contemporary Arts Foundation). It was the mainstay for the art students, and featured a show for many of them. It was housed in an old two story building, and it took a lot of volunteers to keep it going. It was run by an older fellow who cared deeply for contemporary regional art.

When it was time for Mac to have his final graduate show, the director of the CAF arranged for the show to be at a very exclusive restaurant on a small lake in Oklahoma City, call "Christopher's on the Lake".  Mac's large sculptures were placed around the lake.

It was a wonderful show with a beautiful room of hors d'oeuvres.  Most of the array of foods were things Mac had never seen before, like the leaves of the artichoke.  Unfortunately, it sure looked good so he just picked up one of the leaves and ate it, ending up with a mouth full of hard stringy leaf.  When would a country kid from Missouri, with no inside plumbing, ever have eaten the leaf of an artichoke?

Marie was just about as naïve.  Not only did the restaurant provide everything for the opening, but as a wonderful gesture the owner of "Christopher's On The Lake" invited Mac and Marie for a free dinner.  He wanted Mac to see what the restaurant and landscaping was like before the sculpture show.  What a way to see the location, when a simple trip out during the day would have sufficed.  It was a beautiful place with sparkly lights all over the landscape outside, with a circle drive entrance and a valet.  The inside décor was a garden theme with floor to ceiling windows looking out over the lake. Neither Mac or Marie had ever been in a restaurant as fancy as this one.   They were to order anything they wanted on the menu, so they ordered lobster, which neither had ever eaten before.  The meal and service was superb, and the embarrassing part of this story is that they warmly thanked the waiters, but left without knowing they should have given them a tip.

The spring of his graduation, Mac went to the library and wrote down names of about 350 colleges and universities where he thought he might be interested in teaching.  This was the true 'cold calling'.  Letters were sent to each college asking if they had an opening for a sculpture instructor.  Of course that was in the day when there was only a manual typewriter, and each mistake had to be erased by hand and each letter typed individually, all three hundred fifty.   It was a valiant effort but did not produce any openings.  The University Placement department had been sending Mac many openings for art positions in secondary education, but Mac was adamant about only accepting a college position.

In July after graduation, Mac and Marie were blessed with a baby girl, Melissa Marie Hornecker.  They had always wanted three children and were anxious to complete their family and get on with their future.  In fifteen months, they had another wonderful daughter, Marcy Lynn Hornecker.

In the meantime Mac had been working part-time while in school and full-time during the summers in housing construction.  After he graduated from graduate school he started working full-time.  He worked on a great crew with about six guys, most of whom had college degrees.  They were such an intelligent crew and were able to build  high end houses, with elements like elliptical staircases and multiple swimming  pools.  One job, they had was an air-conditioned, climate controlled polo pony barn, which they built before they started on the house.

Once again spring rolled around and Mac started to look for colleges that might have an opening for a sculpture instructor. And once again, the typewriter came out. This time four hundred fifty letters were sent out. As the year went on Mac had several people ask him to build them a house, and he was considering starting his own construction business as he had three houses lined up to build.

One of Mac's fellow students had been very secretive about where he was looking for a job. He and his wife had been good friends of Mac and Marie. One night they came over for a fondue supper and played cards and had a great time. Well, to Mac and Marie's amazement, the next day they separated, and each had a truck that hauled their stuff away. It had all been planned ahead of time. That was the first, and one of the very few, of Mac and Marie's friends to divorced, and it really threw them for a loop.

This fellow classmate was a finalist for the sculptor position at a college, but they decided to not hire him because of the divorce. They contacted the University Placement office again for another candidate. This was about the beginning of July. The placement office sent Mac information about the possible opening and Mac applied not knowing this was the school that had just eliminated his friend. The Dean of Faculty of this college was a very odd Mormon minister. Many of the faculty that he hired were known with time, to be some of the best faculty the college ever had, but he choose them for all the wrong reasons. He flew around and set up interviews with the candidates at their local airports, over a meal.

About this time, Mac had a big professional break. Even though he was putting in long hard hours in construction, he always found time to produce art at night and on weekends. He also continued to show his work and stay active in the art community in Norman and Oklahoma City.

That year following graduation, Oklahoma City commissioned Mac to do a large concrete sculpture to be installed downtown. It weighed many tons and was Mac's first experience needing a crane. The piece was later moved to the lawn in front of the Oklahoma Arts Council. The Arts Council eventually moved to an office building, and the sculpture location is now unknown. As soon as it was installed Mac had large foldout posters of the piece made to use for promotion. Mac immediately sent one to the Dean of Faculty of the college where he had applied. The Dean was so impressed, he moved Mac's application to the top of the pile and arranged an interview at the Oklahoma City airport. This was in July, and the start of the academic year was not far off, so timing was short.

When the Dean interviewed Mac, he also wanted Marie to be there. At that time Mac had a small beard and mutton chop sideburns, looking very country, and Marie was almost seven months pregnant, and they had 2 small children. This was the perfect picture of a country family. The Dean asked Mac to fly to the college for a final interview and they offered him the job. His reason for hiring Mac was that Mac was a good old country boy with a young family. He felt because most of the students that attended his college were from the rural area, within 100 miles , Mac would be able to relate to them. That was the farthest thing from any criteria other deans would have used. In hindsight, the Dean was right, and that was one of the main points that helped make Mac so successful as a teacher and mentor. Mac understood the students and knew that whatever their background, they could be just as successful as anyone else.

Mac didn't spend any time deciding whether to go into the construction business or teach. At that time, he didn't know what kind of teacher he would be, except for the freshman classes he taught at Oklahoma. He just knew he had spent so much of his life involved with art, and that was his passion, so it was a 'no-brainer'.

In less than a month, Mac and Marie, who was now seven and a half months pregnant with Marcy, along with Med and Melissa, packed up all their belongings in a U-Haul and were off to Storm Lake, Iowa and Buena Vista College.

Article - Model Talk

Mac and JR Witt, head of the Contemporary Ats Foundation (CAF), look over one of the models that were on display. The large size sculptures were also on display around a lake at the Oklahoma City restaurant called Christopher's on the Lake

Wood piece on lawn of **7J**, OU's North Base Graduate student art studios

Oklahoma maquettes taken on lawn of **7J**

This was Mac's first large commission and first sculpture requiring cranes. Commissioned by Oklahoma City in 1971 for the downtown area and eventually moved to the lawn in front of the Oklahoma Arts Council.

# SEVEN

## BUENA VISTA COLLEGE (UNIVERSITY)
### Storm Lake, Iowa
September 1971   -   May 2001

Yes, if you have heard anyone pronounce this college name, you would automatically think they were wrong, because they would not be pronouncing it as in Spanish. In Iowa, if you pronounced it just as it looks, with a nasally Buena Vista College, you would be right. As the story has it, Abner Bell, one of the first white men to arrive on the scene, stood on a large rock, peered out over a small lake, and said "Buena Vista" meaning beautiful view, and there you have it. It really is a beautiful place and was home to Mac and his family for thirty years.

Buena Vista College, which was changed years later to Buena Vista University, was and is a small, private, liberal arts college with fewer than twelve hundred main campus students. Of course, that has varied over the years. It is over 100 years old and steeped in tradition. It is, as is the town of Storm Lake, built on the lake by that name. This provides amazing views of the lake from most spots on campus. The beautiful lake, cut out by the glaciers, is very shallow and often wild with whitecaps which gives it its name.

The town of Storm Lake, in the northwest corner of Iowa, is about 70 miles east of Nebraska and South Dakota, and 100 miles south of Minnesota. Sioux City is the closest big town, about 70 miles to the west right on the Iowa-Nebraska line. Storm Lake is a town of about 12,000 people, very agricultural, and the county seat. The land seems very flat but actually is on a large ridge called the Buffalo Ridge. The area is so windy that the largest windmill farm has been built in that area, all the way up the ridge into Minnesota, which makes for a majestic site. Rivers to the west of Storm Lake flow into the Missouri River, and those to the east eventually flow all the way into the Mississippi River. Because of the wind, which averages about thirteen miles per hour, and the northern location, the wind chill temperature can go down to or below minus forty degrees in the winter. Most of the time the lake is frozen over by the end of November, and soon the ice is thick enough to support cars. The snowfall, which usually comes down sideways as a blizzard, is abundant and usually happens in November, and you do not see the ground until sometime in late March. It is a great place to be in the winter if you are young, with the ice skating, snowmobiling, sledding, iceboating, and cross country skiing, to name a few. Of course there are small and large downhill ski areas within driving distance.

When Mac's art friends heard that he was going to accept the position at a college in the northwest corner of Iowa, they were very negative, and described it as the cultural 'art armpit' of the country. They thought the chance that Mac would be able to further his professional art career there, was nil to none. Mac didn't put much stock in needing to be where the 'art action' was to be an artist, and have a successful professional career. If a country kid could shine at JUCO as the school artist, and in the large foundation class at the Kansas City Art Institute, then he could shine in northwest Iowa – and so he did!

It was the last of July when Mac was flown to Storm Lake for the final interview, and offered the sculpture position at the college. He had just one afternoon to find a place for his family to live. At that time there were only three houses available for rent. He chose the best of the three and flew home. The house was a small two bedroom, and soon their third child was to be born. The house was just a few blocks from a large hog processing plant. At night the plant would be unloading the hogs and running them up the ramp to be killed. They would be squealing, and you were sure you could hear them screaming, " help, help me" and warning their fellow hogs below..

Mac and Marie were a little surprised, because of the harsh weather, that so many houses in town had wood exteriors. In Oklahoma, almost all the houses were stone or brick, even though the climate was so much milder. One day, they were just driving around town and looking at the neighborhoods, and both spotted a house they thought was just what they had hoped for. They decided they needed to be looking for different housing and stopped by a realtor. She showed them a couple of houses, and then drove by one that had just been put on the market, but not listed yet. Mac and Marie were in shock!
It was the house they noticed the day before.

It was a three bedroom house, with an 'permastone' exterior, on a nice wooded lot. It actually was in the little town of Lakeside, Iowa, which was on the east end of Storm Lake. They quickly bought it for $18,500 on contract from the owner, and thought they had really stretched their budget. Of course in a few years the housing market skyrocketed, so they really were fortunate to buy when they did. They were so conservative, it was surprising they made such a quick decision. The house was well built and so unique. Every room had two walls of tongue and groove wood, out of knotty pine or plain wood, and the other two walls were high quality vinyl of different solid colors, with the brass decorative nails at the seams. We are talking Unique!

A famous dance hall, restaurant, and cocktail lounge, called the Cobblestone, was down the street on the lake. Actually, all the famous bands had played there many times. In the cocktail lounge the walls were covered with this colored vinyl, and that is where the previous owners got the idea. In the 80's Mac and

Marie added a large screen porch to the east end, which is not visable in the picture, and that is where they spent all their time through the warmer months. Through the years, they were always adding on and remodeling the house, but tried to keep its uniqueness.

Storm Lake home for 30 years, after many projects

The last of October, Marcy was born. Med was now 3 ½, Melissa was 15 months, and now they had a baby, so their children were very close in age. This is exactly what they were hoping for. For a few years, Marie thought she had ruined her life with three small children so close in age, but in a few years, when they got a little older, it was wonderful. The whole family could enjoy doing the same things because the kids were pretty equally capable.

Now they had their three children, which they had wanted, their educations, jobs, and their own home, so life seemed perfect. They were definitely on schedule to not waste time and to make every day count.

When Mac started teaching at Buena Vista College, art was a two man department. The other art professor, Dennis Dykema, had started teaching there just the year before. Dennis was mainly a painter and ceramist and very interested in the administrative end of the college. Mac was principally a sculptor but had done a lot of ceramics and printmaking through his college years, with no interest in the administration or politics of the college. As you can see, they were the perfect odd couple and formed one of the most outstanding art departments of all the colleges and universities in Iowa. They taught together for the next 30 years and retired the same year in May of 2001.

Dennis was very proficient in English and spelling, and Mac definitely was not, as previously noted by needing to take English II three times. They would have so many letters of recommendations and other important papers to write, and Dennis would always check Mac's work. Mac's ideas and composition were well spoken and creatively written, but the spelling and grammar were atrocious. He definitely was a 'right brainer' if there is such a thing. At home, Marie was almost as bad, so could not be of any help. In later years, they would turn to their young son for spelling and grammar questions.

There were some at the college that thought Mac would get farther ahead if he would drop his 'country boy' personality. There were times that he was not included in an event, if there were people involved that the university was trying to impress, but in case they didn't know in advance, he was not going to change. One thing that everyone, everywhere, and at every level, throughout his life, admired about Mac, was the fact that he was true to himself and would not change for anyone or any occasion. What you saw is what you got.

When Mac started teaching, the accepted attire for the professors at BVC was very formal with shirt, nice slacks, sometimes a tie and sport coat. When Mac arrived on the scene, his attire was work shirt and jeans, but mostly overalls. As he always said, he was dressed to work and his work was dirty. From day one the talk and buzz flew around campus about his attire, including some comments to him personally. It really bothered some of the faculty, but as they got to know Mac, they realized that was just Mac, and he kept wearing his overalls. It didn't take long before many of the other professors started dressing a lot more casual.

The Dean of Faculty who hired Mac was a Mormon minister, and very pleasant but very conservative. He was nicknamed "Sneaky Pete" because the rumor was he would snoop around after the faculty left and even go through their trash. This was probably an exaggeration, but it made for good gossip. Also he did not believe in drinking.

The year before Mac began teaching, some of the new young faculty started having faculty parties. Because of the fear of retribution from the Dean, they would not invite any of the non-drinkers, who might 'squeal' and get them in trouble. Reading this today, it seems so overblown, but it was the fact in those times. The parties were barrels of fun, and was one of the reasons the faculty and their spouses became such good friends, regardless of their academic discipline. It was a special time and provided a common feeling of purpose and caring for the institution. Not only were there faculty 'family potluck' picnics, but usually each new faculty wife had a welcome party thrown in her honor by the other faculty wives.

The party problems all changed when a new Dean of Faculty started at the college. The group had the usual 'beginning of school' party, which they asked the new Dean to attend, after they found out that he also 'drank'. It was held at a professor's farm, so very casual and everyone had a good time. Everything was still a little stiff because the President at that time also did not believe in drinking. The time everyone remembers with so much humor, was at the college Christmas faculty and administration dinner party. It was held at a local steak house which has since burned down. Everyone arrived and found their seats and sat down. Then all of a sudden the new Dean got up, and went to the bar, and came back with his Scotch on the Rocks. After a lot of staring in amazement, there was a mass exodus to the bar, and that was the end of BV's prohibition.

   As years went on, and the campus and faculty numbers grew, the faculty wives organization changed into mainly female faculty and staff, and the closeness and comraderie of the total faculty diminished. Faculty members became closer to the colleagues in their own departments, buildings, and committees. But in those early times, the closeness of the faculty and their families was rewarding and became very important.  There were some pretty lean years for the college, and everyone worked together 'for the cause' and did what was necessary to promote, and in the very early years, even save the institution.

   According to Dennis, the curriculum when Mac joined the art department was a mash up of courses; a couple of drawing courses, printmaking, painting, sculpture, and even a crafts course. There was art survey and one history course. There was no articulation to speak of, and students were taking courses far out of sequence.
   One of the first changes Mac and Dennis made was to improve the curriculum by starting a multi hour, two semester foundation sequence, with emphasis on drawing and color, for the freshmen and new art majors. Mac never forgot the importance of the Foundations Class he had at the Art Institute. These two foundations courses at BV were then the prerequisite for the other studio courses, which were Painting, Sculpture, Ceramics, and Printmaking, which Mac and Dennis were able to support with their own expertise.
   A couple of years after Mac started teaching at Buena Vista, the new Dean approved the use of nude models. They always tried to start the first week of classes with a nude model to draw. Mac always said, that set the tone and let the students know they were not in high school art anymore.
   In the Foundations class; during both semesters, they had sections on drawing, painting, ceramics, photography, sculpture, and a few other areas. One was a very intense section on color that seems to be missing in most art department instruction these days. This important section on color used a Color Pak consisting of very pure and intense sheets of every color imaginable. The students were given color problems using the sheets of the Color Pak. Students sometimes worked on the problems for hours or days before coming up with the right combinations, but after completing that section, the students really understood color.
   One student when graduating, gave Mac and Dennis each large portrait paintings of them working. Of course that is the piece of art that all of Mac's children want to inherit. This student's painting was a wonderful example of how well their students understood color. When you are close to the painting it has large brush and palette strokes of paint of the most unusual colors. But, when you stand back, the picture looks almost like a photograph. She certainly learned from her color problems and understood color.

   Finding nude models in a small northwest Iowa town was not an easy thing to do. As luck would have it, the local bowling alley contained a 'strip' bar, which happened to be owned by Mac's next door neighbors.  It was a bar with dancers which would work a circuit and come and go about every week or two. They soon made arrangements with the girls to model during the day for the art classes. About ten in the evening Mac or Dennis would go out to the bar and arrange for one of the dancers to model for the class the next day. Dennis probably handled it easier than Mac, because Mac would nervously be watching his watch until it was time to go procure a model. Walking up to a 'stripper' during her break, and convincing her what you want is on the up and up, was a little hard for an old country boy. Eventually the word was passed on and the girls really enjoyed the extra money. It was also easier money than dancing and stripping, and especially to an audience that gave you respect. The girls stayed in a motel close to Mac's house, so he would stop in the morning, on the way to class, and with a honk at the motel, pick up the girl for that day's class. This probably raised a few of the neighbors eyebrows. A couple of years later the bowling alley burned down and was never rebuilt. Mac and Dennis then found a couple of local women who modeled for them for many years.

Mac, of course, taught sculpture, drawing, and eventually printmaking. Dennis taught painting and ceramics. They each taught all the art history classes, which they initially started with two art history courses, Early Art History taught by Dennis, and Modern taught by Mac. In addition, an art survey class was offered as a general education course.

That curriculum was expanded a few years later with two more art history courses, Ancient and Modern Art History which Mac taught, and Renaissance and Baroque to early 20th century taught by Dennis. They took turns teaching the core Art Survey classes. Each taught the period that they liked best so it was always a positive teaching experience.

Their teaching styles were very different but matched their personalities, and both left their students knowing their art history. Dennis's style was very factual, including dates and locations, while Mac's style was a factual presentation of the art in more of a narrative style, with interesting side stories about the artist or the piece of art. Mac felt this would make a lasting impression on the students and be an interesting way of remembering the art.

Both styles complimented each other for the betterment of the student. Mac's daughter went to BV for two years as an art major. She then transferred to another well-known private college with a very good art history program with multiple art history professors. She found she was much better prepared and much more knowledgeable of art history than the other art history students at that school.

When Mac would go back to BV for events like homecoming, there were always non-art major alums, who would come up and tell him how they enjoy going to art museums because of the good art survey class they took. Imagine, a general education art survey class making a mark on a student's future life experiences. That's the way it is supposed to be, and one of the advantages of a good liberal arts college.

Of course Art Survey was never their favorite class to teach. It became too time consuming for a two man department trying to teach all disciplines. In later years they hired adjunct local artists to teach that class, but nonetheless it was important. Mac tried to start his beginning sculpture class on a project for casting. That excited the students and told them once again that this wasn't high school art. A typical Syllabus for Beginning or Sculpture I, and Advanced or Sculpture II was:

## Sculpture I     Mac Hornecker

This is the study of 3-D design and beginning sculpture.  We will work with real materials – i.e. – plaster, mold making, pattern making, casting in aluminum, and other projects.
From time to time I will give slide talks or refer to books.
Each student should have a sketch book that I can look at from time to time.

I expect students to work outside of class time.  Projects have to be kept on schedule so as not to get behind or you can lose out on casting or other things.   Also, learn the proper use of tools.   You can checkout tools as you need them.

Grades:     You will get a grade for:
        **Attendance** – 3 misses – grade drops a letter – after that each miss drops a grade letter
        **Outside work**  - the more work the higher the grade
        **Your projects** – projects are not graded individually but as a whole
        **Final Project**

Things I look for – quality idea  --- quality of craftsmanship, and --- your understanding of the materials and the process.  --- After you do something, you should be able to teach someone how to do the process.
I am interested in you as an individual artist.  We will work on your communication skills as an artist.


**Project #1**  Modeling – Clay --- waste mold --- casting in concrete
**Project #2**  Piece mold
**Project #3**  Modeling plaster
**Project #4**  Modeling from life --- resin bond sand casting in aluminum
**Project #5**  Lost foam dry sand casting
**Project #6**  Final project

## Sculpture 2    Mac Hornecker

We will spend more time developing you as a sculptor.  There will be a concentration on historical context as applied to modern sculpture.  Each student is expected to concentrate on personal sculptural style and communication.

Grades :  Grades will be determined by commitment and quality of work produced.
Attendance and outside work mandatory

Students should demonstrate knowledge of the following techniques:
- Welding, Gas-Arc, and general iron and metal working techniques
- Woodworking – table saw, band saw, miter box, sanders, skill saw, jig saw, carving, and hand tools
- Advanced casting techniques – we will do a class project in Chinese block casting

I will work with each student to develop and critique works.  Also, I will be available for technical advice. The goal is to produce professional quality sculpture as well as advance personal artistic communication skills.

Mac's teaching style was no nonsense, no bull shit, teach and lead by example. Students would be so excited when they got a thumbs up, a "not bad", or any little positive remark or expression, because they knew, Mac didn't say it was good unless he really meant it. He always appreciated hard work and students who would really try, even if the final result wasn't anything to be proud of. He often gave a better class grade than the work really deserved, to a student who tried his hardest, but Mac would be honest and let them know that their work needed to be better. He always had a soft spot for a responsible student with a really good work ethic.

During the class and especially at the end of each semester there would be a critique. The students would gather around their work and Dennis and Mac would critique, praise, and criticize their pieces. The students would also critique each other's work. At times, it seemed brutal, and at times, there would be tears, because they were all very blunt, which they had been taught to do. It was a valuable learning experience. To be an artist, you have to build up a thick skin, because you will have a lot of negative input about your work, no matter how famous you become.

In 1977, Mac won a competitive sculpture commission at the South Dakota Memorial Art Center. The piece was called 'Prairie Bluff', 16' x 16' x 32' long, of steel, stone, and concrete. It was a very geometric, innocuous piece that should not have offended anyone. But as Mac was standing in front of the piece giving an interview to a TV reporter, with cameras rolling, a man came up and started hitting him over the head with a rolled up newspaper. Everyone was stunned and didn't know what to say or do, but that was one of the first of many 'art critics' and where 'thick skin' comes in handy.

Actually everyone looked forward to the critiques at the end of the semesters because after the critiques, everyone would go to Dennis's or Mac's house for supper and a party.

Dennis's dinner was his famous special homemade chili after the fall semester critique, and Mac would fix a Cajun feast after the spring semester. In the early years, Mac and Dennis's wives would help with snacks and hors d'oeuvre , or as Mac laughingly would say 'hordy dovers'. The guys soon put a stop to their fancy help and declared they would do it all. Since these parties lasted for the 30 years, that turned out to be a gift.

They were great cooks, and the students still talk about Mac and Dennis's parties, as one of their fondest memories of college at BV. Mac's menu was always Red Beans and Rice with Hot Sausage links; Cajun Hot Slaw; big homemade bread loafs split and broiled and lathered with butter and cheeses; and Cajun fried rice cakes, that were fried drop donuts with boiled rice in the batter. Mac's cooking hero was Justin Wilson. Mac watched his cooking show during the years in Oklahoma, while watching the kids, and loved his cookbook.

At Mac's house, they would usually migrate outside to a fire pit. Mac and several of the students would pull out their guitars and sing, and as the night went on there would be a lot of philosophizing under the stars. It was always a great group.

The students who were of age could bring their drinks of choice, if they didn't want pop, but they never got really drunk or caused a scene. They were also good about having the clear-headed ones drive back to the dorm, which was about three miles around the lake. Some were known to walk back to the dorm. The parties were so valuable, because it got the upper and lower classmen together to have fun, and get to know each other well.  Many of the students became good friends, regardless of their class rank, because they developed as artists together.

Mac always had his beloved old country western music playing in the studio, so through time he had converted a lot of the students, and they knew all the words.  Mac knew and played his guitar to hundreds of those old songs.  The only problem, which became a joke, was that once he was on a 'roll' you couldn't get him to stop.  The songs just kept rolling out of his head, sometimes into the late hours and he would keep saying, " Oh, just one more".   Along with the music playing during the studio classes, he often had Sassafras root boiling in a pan of water on the hot plate.  He was always digging up the root when he visited the family farm in southern Missouri.   It produced a neat smell and was good to drink like sarsaparilla, which was a little bit more touch of ' country'.

Of course, in the days when Dennis and Mac taught art history classes, they used slides.  Mac made a huge lighted slide case in the painting studio.  By the slide case  were always some old comfy well used chairs and a couch or two.   The students would hang out there, studying the slides and just being together having a good time.   This also promoted so much comraderie between the students, and fun memories they never forgot.

Just before class, Mac and Dennis would go to the slide case, pull out the slides for the next lecture, put them into their projector cartridge, and then return them after class.  The students could then study them at their leisure or when they wanted to just 'hand out' together in the painting studio.  Of course now, all the images are put on the computer and each student can study them from home or in their dorm rooms.  It just seems like there is something that was lost in this modern computerized world, but it is now a lot easier for the professors.

Buena Vista, now a university, was the first school to give each new freshman a new laptop computer, and made the campus all wireless.  At that time it was a really big deal, because most students couldn't afford a computer, and would have to go to the computer centers on campus.  Everyone starting off with a laptop at a wireless campus,  meant that students could take their computer to class, to their dorm room, or down by the lake, to sit and study.   Now with multiple computers and laptops in most households, it is hard to believe that getting a free laptop as a freshman, could be a deciding factor for choosing a college.   But that was one of the schools reasons, complete with a national television ad together with Gateway, Inc., the Sioux City based computer company.

Mac loved for his students to have outside jobs or get married.  It would force them to schedule their time better and not waste it.  When they got married, they seemed to get serious about their future.  That view did not always work, but many times it did, and the perfect example of success was based on Mac's own past.

Mac stayed very active professionally, for the 30 years he taught at BV.  While teaching there and after retirement, Mac's pieces were acquired by over 30 permanent public collections of which six were direct commission requests and four were competitive commissions. He had over 25 solo shows, over 50 group shows, was accepted into over 25 invitational shows, and was chosen to be in over 30 competitive shows. He won several awards, an Artist in Residence, and over six times was a guest artist.

Mac had great support from the university, and especially from the former President, during of his long tenure. The former President provided a large commissioned sculpture of Mac's for the campus when Mac retired. Also, the university was always happy to have Mac set pieces around campus, along with student work.

This may sound trivial, but most universities will not allow that except around the art department, and when you do install a piece, you have to jump through so many hoops. You soon find out that you are dealing with a lot of 'chiefs' that should only be Indians'. Not only do you need to get permission from the school, but also from those in charge of the grounds, and landscaping, and it goes on and on.

Years later while teaching in Arkansas, an older student who was actually a long time professor of visual arts and English at another university, took all of Mac's sculpture classes. This student had a sabbatical, which he dedicated to building sculpture, and had a sabbatical show on his campus. He displayed one large outside piece on Mac's campus with the good graces of Mac's university. He then moved that tall linear piece to the front of the building on his campus, where his ' sabbatical art show' was being shown. It looked very nice and really complemented the building and landscape, but shortly after the show was over, he was told to take in down. He was surprised and Mac was furious. Well, he removed the sculpture and returned it to the campus of Mac's school where it was welcomed and has stayed for years. This is more the norm than one might expect. Heaven forbid that the liberal arts educated students would be exposed to art!

Mac was affiliated with several galleries in other major cities, but the Olson Larsen Gallery in West Des Moines, Iowa was his main gallery. He was very fortunate to have become affiliated with them. The gallery was established in 1970 as one of the first galleries in the area to promote regional artists. The gallery changed owners in 1979 when it was bought by Marlene Olson and Ann Larsen and became the Olson Larsen Gallery. Mac join the gallery's 'stable' of artists shortly after Marlene Olson became the sole owner in 1984. The gallery is in the old historic downtown area of West Des Moines called Valley Junction, which had been revitalized and contained many unique businesses. Marlene continued to use the same gallery name and represented regional artists or those with regional connections. Marlene built up a very large corporate clientele and most of Mac's large commissions, all over the state of Iowa, were through the efforts of her gallery. Marlene sold the gallery in 2010, to Susan Watts who had managed the gallery for the last 7 years, so is continuing in much the same way as before.

In the early years, Mac had several important pieces, but he also entered every professional art show or possible commission he heard about. His selection would be through an elimination process from a committee or a juror. The selection process for a commission usually consisted of Mac submitting a proposal and drawings. Hopefully he would be selected as one of a smaller group of entrants, sometimes as few as three finalists. At that time, he would build a maquette and give a presentation. If he was selected, after the contract was signed, he would start building and usually have the piece ready, way before the contractual installation time.

If the project was in the Des Moines area, or Mac had been informed of a project around the state or area by Olson Larsen Gallery, they would ask Mac if he was interested and send him all the site information.  If he was interested, the gallery would enter, on this behalf, the information required, such as, examples of his major works and a statement.  If he was chosen as a finalist, Mac would make a maquette to be presented by him or the gallery or both.  If his piece was chosen, the gallery would write up the contracts and manage all the business connected with the piece, so Mac could just be an artist and fabricate and install.

 Later in Mac's professional career, the clients would contact the gallery and just want a" Mac Hornecker'. At that time, he would go see the site, design a sculpture, and make a maquette, which was presented to the client for approval.  It was usually always accepted, and then the gallery would take care of the contracts, signing, and payments.  Mac never started a commission until the contract was signed, which was a lesson some of his friends learned the hard way.   Marlene always insisted on a stipend for her artists before they would work on a proposal and presentation. That is not always the case.   Many times Mac met with interested people that had contacted a gallery, traveled to check out sites, and even made drawings and maquettes, for the people to finally say, "I will think about it.".  This was just another way of saying, " I am not interested" and he would never hear from them again.  Of course, Mac usually knew from the beginning they were not really serious.  When interested clients put down good money, you are assured they are serious.  If they don't like your idea, they tell you so, and you are happy to return with another proposal.  With Marlene, the artist was treated like a true professional.

In the art world now, it is standard for a gallery to charge 50 percent of the selling price for any piece they sell.  Most of the time, artists sign an exclusive contract with the gallery, which encompasses a certain area, usually in miles around the gallery.  Because of this arrangement, the gallery works harder to sell the artist's work, and has exhibitions at the gallery to showcase their work.  Mac's gallery charged a smaller percentage for his large sculpture pieces, because of the added cost of building, transportation, installation, and higher selling price.  For  any commissioned piece of art, Mac's contract always required payment of one-third at the beginning after signing the contract, one-third half way through the time set for installation, and the last third after the piece was installed.  This was the contract that Olson Larsen Gallery used but probably is pretty universal.

Marlene and Mac, had a wonderful relationship and she understood that he did not enjoy the business end of being an artist, so she did everything for him, and had him very spoiled.

Mac always loved slides.  He was always behind in the latest technology and would drag his feet to modernize.  He truly did not think that this new digital photography was even close to the image he could get from slides.  One day Marlene quietly hinted to Marie that Mac was the gallery's only artist who still used slides.  Of course digital images were so much easier to work with.  Marlene sometimes funneled her wants through Marie to ease the new idea to Mac, and he would change before he knew what hit him.

As stated, in the beginning of his professional years, Mac entered most sculpture commission competition or professional art shows that he heard of. Some shows would be far away, but most would be in the Midwest. Besides sculpture, Mac, in his earlier professional years, would submit drawings, prints, and ceramics; anything he felt he had an expertise and had any current work.

As time went by, Mac's sculptures commanded a much higher price. It is surprising to look at his early installed pieces and realize the small amount of money Mac received. In those days he was glad, to just break even, and have a chance to build a piece and have his work appreciated, He just wanted to make art.

Mac was fortunate to have a job in the area that he loved. His job and professional career all meshed together. Most artist have a job to support their art, and have to work on their art in their spare time. Many times the artists are forced to prostitute their art to be able to pay their bills. Mac was always elated to sell a piece or get a commission, but if it didn't happen, it did not present a personal financial tragedy, which gave him a lot of artistic freedom.

Also, Mac's drawings were wonderful and prolific. He drew fast, whether on a large or small piece of paper, with his drawing hand in constant motion. One time, he followed a creek from close to its beginning until it emptied into Storm Lake, and then as it left the lake. He drew the view from both sides of each bridge that crossed the creek, with each drawing being 22"x30". Surprisingly, all the drawings are totally different landscape images and show the diversity of what most think of as plain, flat, land. He called the series of drawings "From The Bridge" and showed the project several times putting the drawings end to end in sequence that measured 96 feet. He also loved drawing the human form.

Mac's sculptures were always preceded by a lot of drawings of ideas. The size and difficulty of fabricating Mac's sculptures also required a lot of technical and precise drawings. Elements had to fit perfectly, be level to fit a footing at precisely the right place, and be safe. Mac's pieces were all modular and bolted together, which left no place for error. When the sculptures were installed, the elements with the holes and brackets to bolt the pieces together had to come together exactly right.

Also, concrete footings had to be poured, but designed exactly where the elements of the piece would be. Each piece and location required a different type and design of concrete footing, based on frost/freeze depths, and weight and size of the piece to be bolted to the concrete footing. In his early years, Mac would even do all his concrete work, but as time went on, and the footing size increased dramatically, he handed the technical blueprints over to concrete contractors to construct the footings ahead of the installation. Mac had enough to do before the crane and sculpture arrived. Many times the sculpture elements had to be transported to the site by a semi-truck. At the beginning of the installation the timing had to be perfect so the crane would be on site to unload the semi. The semi was on a tight schedule and the crane was being paid by the hour.

Of course many of Mac's sculpture presentations had a maquette, but would also include drawings. During his earlier presentations, most of Mac's drawings were airbrush drawings, which with computerization, is a lost art. Most of his earlier finished drawings of sculpture ideas were also airbrushed.

## Airbrush drawings of sculpture ideas

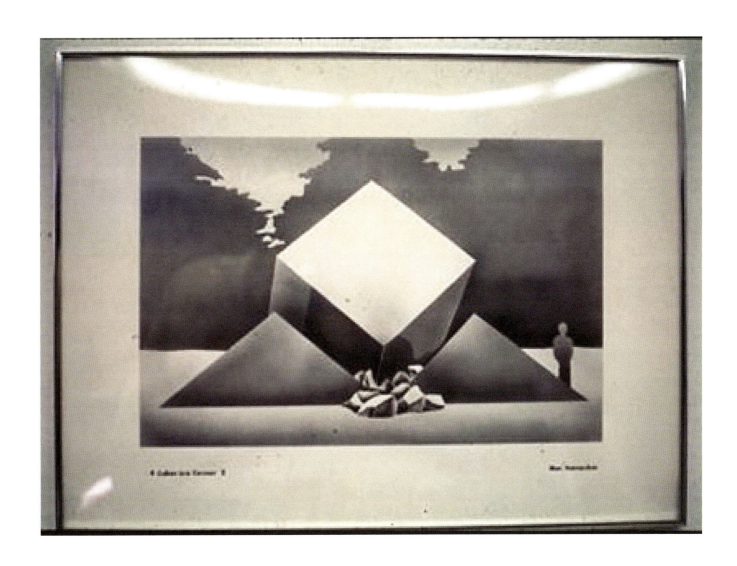

# Drawings of ideas for sculptures

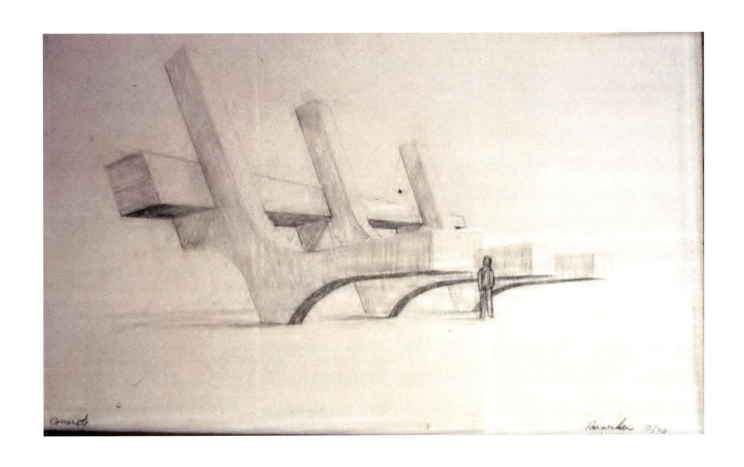

In the summer of 1976, Mac was a guest artist at the Kansas City Art Institute. This was a thrilling time for Mac. One day, three of his friends who lived in his little home town, visited Mac at the Art Institute. They remarked that Mac's home town should have a piece of his work.

While teaching there, Mac made a piece of sculpture called MO Bluff, about 60' x 8' x 6', of welded steel, concrete, and rock. Mac told his friends that they could have the piece, if they could find a way to get it to Sheldon, which was about one hundred miles south. He also told them that he would install it. He suggested they write to the Missouri Arts Council for money. They did write a grant asking for $1500. One day, the Arts Council called Mac and wanted to know if it was for real, this small town wanted a major piece of sculpture. He told them it was definitely true, so they sent them $3000.

Since they received more money than they asked for, Mac offered to put in concrete sidewalks to and through the sculpture, with concrete benches. Marie and a friend landscaped around the sidewalks to make a little park.

June of 1977, Mac arrived in Sheldon to install the sculpture. It was to be placed in one corner of the square block park area, in the center of town. The block park was bordered by a community building, covered stage, a playground, and contained a ball field. It was definitely the center of town activity and the annual Old Settlers Picnic.

The night before the big installation, Mac put on a slide show at the covered stage. When the time arrived, people came from all directions with their lawn chairs for the program. Mac explained how he made sculptures, his thought process, and about how his work was influenced by all the landscapes that he had grown up with around that area. He also invited everyone to come the next day to help install the sculpture.

The next day was a Hoot! The older ladies from the apartment complex across the street, affectionately called 'Wrinkle Village" by the locals, also helped. Seeing them pushing wheelbarrows of dirt away in their housedresses with their white plastic purses still hanging on their arm, was a sight to behold. There was a lot of help and was something they could take a lot of proud in, because they were a part of this thing called 'a sculpture'.

It was a long and linear piece with Osha Yellow painted vertical I-beams that raised up in the center and then down into a formed bed of rocks to proceed again with a linear element. The piece was raised on concrete footings, so the long elements were a couple feet off the ground.

What made the project most rewarding was at night the locals would walk to the sculpture from all directions of the town, carrying their lawn chairs. They would sat around the sculpture and on the long elements, like birds on a clothes line, and visited until dark.

In 2012 the sculpture was repainted and a more extensive landscaped park was established. The town had repainted the sculpture many times but the landscaping was gone. Now it is an introduction to a whole new generation to the art form of sculpture. It is now common to see kids sitting and climbing on the sculpture and adults setting on the concrete benches. In the summer of 2012, two weddings were held under the sculpture.

**MO BLUFF**  1977
painted steel, rock, and concrete
60' x 8' x 6'
Sheldon, Missouri (Mac's home town)

In 1977, Mac sold a large piece to Pacesetter, a company in Omaha, Nebraska. Mac also had the good fortune to start showing in Omaha, Nebraska at a unique gallery called Gallery 72. This was a very ordinary 'store front' looking building, along a street in Omaha, owned and operated by one of the most interesting couples, Bob and Roberta Rogers. They were an old couple, who lived above the art gallery and had an amazing art clientele. Bob had retired from owning several Donut Shops, and after retirement they lived, ate, and breathed art. One of their sons had gone to an art institute. Their tiny apartment was wall to wall wonderful art. It consisted of a living room, and a kitchen with a bedroom partitioned off with a half wall. The apartment had a huge table in the center of the kitchen, piled high with art magazines, and a cup of Roberta's very strong coffee would be waiting for you, served with a smile and very strong southern accent. The night before every opening, they would have a potluck supper of the most incredible food, with artists and art patrons in the little apartment. Everyone looked forward to these evenings and drove from miles around to attend. Bob and Roberta ran the gallery and climbed those stairs well into their eighties and nineties. After their deaths, one of their sons, who has retirement, opened Gallery 72 again. It is in a new location on historic Vinton St. in Omaha.

The piece that was bought by Pacesetter in Omaha, sat on the BV campus originally for a few years. It was always the target for student pranks. One time the students painted dots on the cube so it looked like a die, which Mac thought was clever and was easy to paint over. It was used a lot for group or club pictures with people on the ground and also perched on the horizontal beams. Mac has always thought it was fine for adults to sit on his sculptures and for kids to play on them. That was the public interacting with art.

**YELLOW ONE**  1977
Pacesetter Corporation , Omaha, Nebraska
steel   7' x 16' x 12'
(Pacesetter Corporation has since closed and they donated the piece
to Buena Vista University, where it proudly stands by the new art department)

**PRAIRIE BLUFF** 1979
steel, rock, and concrete
South Dakota Memorial Art Center
Brookings, South Dakota
National Sculpture Competition II

    In 1979, Mac entered and won the National Sculpture Competition II conducted by the South Dakota Memorial Art Center in Brookings, South Dakota. The piece was called 'Prairie Bluff'. This was another professional breakthrough. With some of the money from selling the sculpture, Mac was able to buy a 20 foot flatbed gooseneck trailer, so he had a way of hauling this and other large pieces of sculpture. He pulled the trailer with his 1971 ¾ ton International pickup truck, which was his prize possession, called Bertha. He was a happy sculptor.

**ALIGNED LANDSCAPE** 1980
Corten steel, concrete
14' x 34' x 10'

Commissioned by Northwestern University
Orange City, Iowa

    Mac continued to work big.  Finding a place to fabricate the large pieces was always a dilemma.  One would find Mac on several occasions cording off an area of the faculty parking lot, grinding and welding away for all to see.  In 1984,  he made a piece in the parking lot,  called  MO River.  It was made from Corten and native rock, 9' x 16' x 18'h and was installed at Bellevue College, in Bellevue, Nebraska..

**MO RIVER** 1984
Corten steel, rock, and concrete
9' x 16' x 18   Commissioned by
Bellevue College
Bellevue, Nebraska

During the 80's, Mac was always producing art, but unless he had a commission, his pieces had to be on a much smaller scale, due to the cost. On a family trip to Minneapolis, Minnesota Zoo, Mac noticed a new outside area being built for the lions. The zoo was in the process of making the rocks and bluffs out of cement and were staining them to look very real. Mac noticed a sculptor working with the crew that he had met before, so he made a point to talk to the sculptor, and inquire about the technique and where they got their stains. Now concrete staining is so common, but then it was a real specialty, and the stains, that actually made a chemical reaction with the concrete, had to be ordered from California. Mac returned home and immediately started designing, building, and incorporating man-made rocks into his sculptures. Of course they were hollow, so much lighter, and needed to be strongly built with steel armatures. It took lots of practice to make them look real and not like a gigantic, as Mac would say, " turd". Because they were so well-built, over twenty five years later they look like they did the day they were installed, only better because they have aged and sometimes even grow lichens. Sculptures of steel and steel rocks, or steel and man-made rocks, became Mac's signature style.

**ROCKET** 1988
steel and ferroconcrete
4' x 6' x 7'

**SQUEEZE** 1985
steel and ferroconcrete
17' x 10' x 6'

**BUTTRESS** 1985
steel and ferroconcrete
10' x 5' x 5'

**DO-DAH DANCER** 1987
steel and ferroconcrete
6' x 4' x 7'

**SPLASH** 1992
steel and ferroconcrete
10' x 6' x 7'

**ICE** 1994
steel and ferroconcrete
8' x 6' x 3'

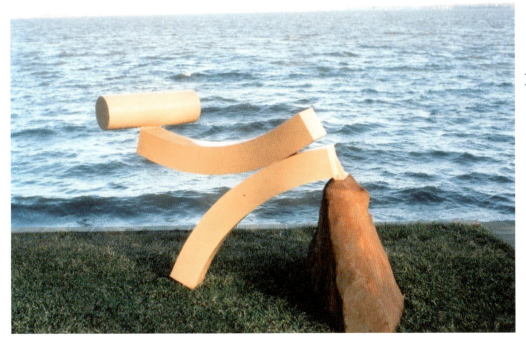

**LOESS** 1995
steel and
ferroconcrete
6' x 5' x 9'

**GETTY** 1996
steel and ferroconcrete
8' x 6' x 8'

maquette

maquette
aluminum and stone

**Mac's first studio, what a beauty!!**
He couldn't have been more excited
Who said you need a fancy studio to make good art

 

    In 1988, Mac rented an abandoned large concrete warehouse close to his house. The building had been a camphor factory during World War I, and was used last to manufacture caskets. It had been empty for many years. It was mainly a concrete shell, with two story ceilings, and home to hundreds of pigeons. Mac and his friends spent many days shooting pigeons and trying to convince them to leave for the new inhabitant. Mac paid thirty dollars a month rent, which sounds pretty cheap, but the building was unheated, had no running water, and the roof leaked. Mac was so proud to have his first real studio. Of course, everything had to be covered with plastic to protect his equipment and to keep the work dry, so the steel would not rust.

The first big sculpture Mac made in the 'new' studio was a piece commissioned by Farm Bureau of Iowa to be installed in 1989. It was to be placed in their large atrium of the Iowa corporate office in West DesMoines, Iowa, and was called 'River'. River was a beautiful piece, measuring 12' x 50' x 12' of welded steel. Mac used his signature patina which was then covered with wax. The river elements were smooth steel but Mac always welded the rocks with many planes and angles and then finished them by welding texture onto the surface. This finish for his sculpture was only for indoor installations, but had a beautiful, dark, rich gunmetal appearance.

**RIVER** 1989
welded steel
12' x 50' x 12'
Farm Bureau of Iowa, West Des Mnoies

Erection Crew for RIVER

View of RIVER
from upper
walkway in
Iowa Farm Bureau
West DesMoines, IA

About this time, all Mac's friends started getting involved with the process. There would be daily visits to his studio to check the progress, and they were there in full force to help with the installation wherever it happened to be. Mac had a wonderful mix of friends, including the owner of the local sanitation service, a writer, an owner of a farm management business, a dentist, and a grocer. They proudly became known as Mac's Erection Crew. Of course there were many others who checked on the daily progress, and probably started to enjoy, and have a special feeling, for the art of sculpture.

In 1994, Mac purchased a lot, about three-fourths of an acre, in the light industrial area in Storm Lake. It was really handy, because it was about one mile from his house. He then had a large metal building built on the site for a studio. Mac lost the use of the concrete warehouse when the owner raised the rent, but really wanted it for his own use. It actually was a good thing, because it forced Mac to build a really good studio for himself, which was a dream come true. Mac had always been so financially conservative and was brought up to make do with what he had. It was so hard for him to make that step, but he was one excited sculptor.

Mac's new studio building was 36'x50' which included a 12'x 36' air conditioned/heated space with a full bathroom, which was required by code. It was quite tall and had two large sliding doors that would allow for tall and wide structures to be moved in and out. There was a large concrete slab in front of the building, so Mac could work outside during nice weather.

Mac had traded a sculpture, with one of the members of his Erection Crew, for a one car garage that he was wanting to replace. Getting it moved across town and on the lot turned out to be another Erection Crew experience.

Of course there was also plenty of space to set large sculptures around, but the most important spot was his watermelon patch. During the summer, the fun was having friends stop by to check on the sculpture progress and eat a watermelon from the garden. Since Mac was always a frustrated farmer with no place to have a garden, this was a perk of having his studio. He grew all the normal garden plants but also had a wonderful rhubarb and asparagus patch.

Asparagus grew wild in that area, especially along fence rows where birds have deposited the seed. Everyone had certain places they liked to hunt for asparagus, but it was always first come first serve, and on Sundays you had to beat the church crowd. Mac's favorite place was the fence row along the railroad tracks. Most years Mac and Marie would put up to 40 quarts of asparagus in their freezer. When they first moved to Storm Lake, they thought they would only be there for a few years. They didn't want to plant asparagus, which takes a few years to get established. Well after thirty years, they sure wish they had. When Mac built the studio, he dug up some of the asparagus he had been picking along the railroad tracks and planted it in the garden, so he had a great patch from then on.

Rhubarb pie was his favorite dessert, so the rhubarb really got used. Mac was famous for his rhubarb rolls, and it was always the request of his kids and grandkids on every visit. Actually rhubarb is a bumper crop in that part of the country, and many people used it as a landscaping plant because of its big leaves and thick growth.

The garden for Mac was like meditation is for others. He would work awhile and then go out and hoe and think. His garden was always free of weeds, and probably a lot of sculpture ideas were realized there.


As the studio building was being erected, Mac, who had worked in construction most of his life, worked along with the crew. One day, Mac was headed home for lunch and started having cold sweats and shallow breathing. He knew immediately he was having a heart attack. Luckily his home was only a mile away. When he got home, he called the next door neighbor, who had just recovered from bypass heart surgery and carried Nitroglycerin. The neighbor, came over and immediately gave him some nitro, and took him to the hospital.

Marie was working at a pharmacy in a town about twenty miles away. The hospital called her and the doctor kept her informed while the pharmacy staff tried to find another pharmacist to come and relieve her.  The doctor finally decided to air flight Mac to Sioux City, and Marie arrived in Sioux City just as the helicopter landed.

They ended up performing an angioplasty, and in a couple of days Mac was like new.  He had a blockage, but probably the most important thing that happened, was the neighbor immediately giving him the Nitro to help open the artery, so there was minimal damage.  Mac was one of the lucky ones who got a warning, especially in light of all his family history and uncles that did not make it to 50.

The studio was built and was a hot place for many years.  Actually it still is a hot place.  Several years after Mac and Marie moved to Arkansas, one of the local mortuaries asked to buy the property for a crematorium! The town had a newer large population of immigrants from Laos and Hispanics from Mexico because of the IBP pork packing plant.  The Laotians believed in cremation and the burning of the body was part of the funeral ceremony observed by all.  The Hispanics cremated the body so it could be taken back to Mexico.  For the Laotian's cremation ceremonies, they redecorated the apartment area of the studio and even added a large viewing window into the Retort room.  There was not another crematorium for one hundred miles. There had been a car accident from the long line of mourners following a body to the crematorium, so the local mortician thought they needed a place in Storm Lake. Mac and Marie had been using the studio as a convenient place to stay when they went back to visit in Storm Lake.  The mortuary owner, who had been a 'frequent sculpture building watcher and watermelon eater',  decided they would like to buy Mac's studio instead of building a new facility.  It was a surprise, but he made a good offer.  Mac always joked that he made a mistake by not putting a free burn into the contract.

The studio gave Mac the advantage of space for very large works to be built.  In 1996, Mac was commissioned to build a large piece for the lobby of the EMC or Employers Mutual Company insurance building in downtown DesMoines.  It was called Prairie Wind of welded steel, and was 16' x 30' x 14'.  It was a beautiful piece that could be admired by all passersby through the two story windows looking out over a main downtown street and from a catwalk over the street into the building.

**PRAIRIE WIND** 1996
welded steel
15' x 30' x 15'
Employers Mutual Company
Des Moines, Iowa

Erection Crew for
PRAIRIE WIND

Erection Crew at work- view from public crosswalk

During these years Mac did a lot of work in laminated wood, using a great deal of oak, walnut and mahogany, and often incorporated wooden chains into the pieces. He never wanted to be known for his wood pieces, but they are in many private and corporate collections. In 1997, two pieces, 'Tornado Struck' and 'Up the Creek', were bought for the foyer of the magnificent Hotel Pattee in Perry, Iowa, a town close to Des Moines. This was a grand old hotel that was once empty, but completely refurbished by a philanthropist from California. She had been raised in Perry and wanted to give back to the town. The Hotel Pattee was run like a five star hotel with a European chef and every amenity one could imagine. But the most important pleasure for the eyes of the hotel clients, was the enormous amount of original, regional art in every nook, room, stairway, and hallway.

In the same year, the hotel owner commissioned Mac to do a collection of rock sculptures hanging on the tall brick wall that rimmed the roof. This wall was the view from the windows of just eight rooms. Every room had a different theme relating to an important historical event or person of the area, with a different interior designer for each room. The Hotel was an amazing place and so special because of all the wonderful original regional art.

**Prairie Markers**  1997
ferroconcrete
Hotel Pattee, Perry, IA

**TORNADO STRUCK**
wood
84" x 38" x 12"
Hotel Pattee, Perry, IA
Photo by Ellen Bak
for book Lit By The Sun

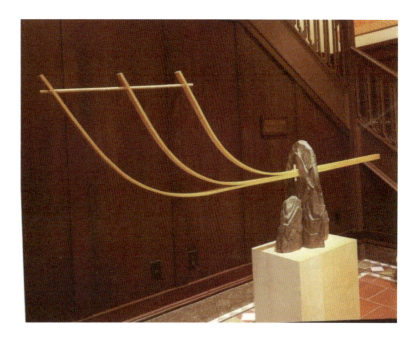

**UP THE CREEK**
wood
51" x 38" x 16 "
Hotel Pattee, Perry, IA
Photo by Ellen Bak
for book Lit By the Sun

**WOOD GARDEN**
1997
Wood
12' x 12' diameter
Piece created for the first show in the new Sioux City Art Center in Sioux City, Iowa

In 1997, the graduating class at the Pennsylvania College of Optometry, bought one of Mac's wood pieces for a gift to the school. The sculpture was mahogany 34" x 72"x 32", called CAUTION TO THE WIND

**CAUTION TO THE WIND**
wood, Mahogany
34" x 72" x 32"
Pennsylvania College of Optometry
Salus University, Elkins Park, PA

**HOOPDI DO**
Laminated wood
6' x 6' x 3'

**HAMMER**
wood, Oak
33" x 31" x 9"

**OUTSIDE THE LOOP** 1999
wood, oak
51" x 24" x 13"

**TIME OUT** 1999
wood, Oak
43" x 30" x 32"

**EL NINO** 1998
steel and ferroconcrete
8' x 7' x 14'

**SNAIL** 1998
steel and ferroconcrete
8' x 8' x 14'

**BRONKO**   1993
steel and ferroconcrete
7' x 14' x 7'
Henderson State University
Arkadelphia, Arkansas


   BV gave the faculty chances for a great deal of foreign experiences.  The school started an exchange program with a province in China.  The exchange was for six Buena Vista faculty to go to China for three weeks as the guest of Hubei Province.  They were treated royally and were shown China from Beijing to Hong Kong.  In exchange for this wonderful trip, China would send one professor to Buena Vista for a full school year. The first group of BV professors, which included Mac, went to China in January, which was very cold.  It was a year before the Tiananmen Square disaster.  China was a much different, tighter, and less modern place, than it is now.  In some ways, it was wonderful that BV professors were able to see China before the transformation, but they were never allowed to go out on their own and were always very supervised.  The following year, the group decided to go in May for warmer weather, and they found they were able to move around on their own much more.  All went well that second year, except they arrived in Beijing just as Tiananmen Square was erupting. They were promptly moved to a new resort with no idea why, and Buena Vista did not know where they were, which caused a few nervous days.  One has to realize that you are dealing with a different culture, but it was a golden opportunity for a poor farm boy from the hills of Missouri.

One of their young guides was very curious about their life in America.  One day he ask Mac , "Do you have car?" Well at the time he had 3 kids that needed transportation and of coarse Mac and Marie, so they had five junk cars with each over one hundred thousand miles.  When Mac told them he had five cars, he was astonished and said, " 5 CARS!"  It sounded pretty good but little did he know what condition they were in. The guide later came to America and did not go back.  His wife was allowed to come but without their son to insure that she would come back which she did not.  They eventually were able to be reunited with their son.

Mac also had more opportunities to see the world because of programs at the university.  The school was on a fall semester, a month interim in January, and spring semester schedule.   During the interim month, students took one class taught around a special theme,  if they stayed on campus, or they could go on an extensive trip.  Many trips were offered, emphasizing different subjects all over the United States and abroad.

One year Mac and a biology professor teamed up to take a group of students on a trip to Guatemala and Belize.  They were great traveling companions. The trip took them to the Mayan Pyramid site of Tikal, in Guatemala;  a week living in the jungle with a native tribe, studying their culture and experimenting on vampire bat; and a week on a small cay to study  and experience the Caribbean in a primitive way.  One of Mac's interests was Mayan art, ever since he had studied it at the Art Institute.  Going to Tikal was a thrill, especially to be able to share the exciting experience with students.

They were a great bunch of students and good sports.   It was not a plush vacation.  They slept many nights in string hammocks with the hogs roaming around them; jungle heat and humidity causing their cloths to mildew while on their back; and riding in trucks on deep muddy roads  barely navigable, to name just a few of their experiences. But the week they were on a cay 'studying marine life' and eating fresh fish and seafood,  snorkeling, and sailing in the beautiful Caribbean, was an enviable, pleasant part of the trip.

Later Mac and Marie took a two week trip to Mexico with friends. The husband was a fellow sculptor and scholar of Mayan art and his wife was a Spanish professor.  They were joining her class trip, but the four of them spent the two weeks immersing themselves in the Mayan culture.   They added Chechen Itza, Uxmal, and Kabah, and the multiethnic site of Teotihuacan, and the wonderful Mayan museums in Mexico City, to their personal Mayan experiences. Of course in those days you could walk or climb up to all the parts of the sites. In later visits, they discovered you could not get close to the sites, let alone touch or climb on them. Also the walls of carvings had deteriorated so much in just a few short years, that some were now hard to make out. Mac was fortunate that he was able to see them while they were in such good shape and detail.

El Castillo in background-Temple of Warriors in far background. You were allowed to climb to top of El Castillo, or through a little side door at the bottom, climb narrow rock stairs inside pyramid, to the red painted Jaguar, with inlays of jade and bone. Now, the temple is barricaded at ground level.

Chac Mool, on top of Temple of Warriors. At that time, you could climb up the stairs and see the Chac Mool up close. Now, that is not allowed and because of the angle from the ground, it cannot be seen.

One of Mac's last ancient art adventures was a trip that Mac and Marie took with their son Med and his wife Beth, to Crete. They all stayed at a villa in a little village about one-third mile up the hill overlooking the sea. They were the only Americans in the villas, which were occupied mainly with Aussies and Brits.
The Aussies and Brits were there for a calm, peaceful holiday, so there was not a frantic, touristy atmosphere. While in Crete, they visited the Palace of Knossos and the Archaeological Museum of Herakleion. Imagine what a thrill this was for Mac since this is all from the Minoan Period which is Pre-Greek and Pre-Roman. In the museum, nothing is behind glass or ropes. You can get inches away from all the exhibits like the famous

snake goddess "Goddess of Appearance", and decorated four and five foot tall vessels that were hand thrown on a wheel. What a wonderful vacation, an education, and more Memories.

In Mexico:
Mac climbing Pyramid
of the Magician at Uxmal-
walking down is 'white knuckle
 time

near Mexico City: At Teotihuacan, friend on Mac's shoulders
to get the primo picture of the stripped jaguar in
the mural along the Avenue of the Dead

    The other great opportunity for another foreign experience was a three week trip to Europe. Of course, the catch is that it was a student trip, but still a wonderful adventure. Their daughter, Marcy, was an art student at the time and she and Marie went along as well. The trip itinerary was Amsterdam, Munich, Oberammergau, Rome, Pompeii, Paris, Geneva, and London. The trip stayed in most cities for 3 days and everyone had Euro Passes for the train. The students could go anywhere they wanted as long as they traveled with at least another student, but they usually explored in groups. They had to be in their hotel at night and they traveled from city to city together on the train. They did a lot of sightseeing as one big group, but showed a lot of maturity and independence to go to special things they were interested in seeing. It was a culture trip and introduction to foreign travel and major places in Europe. They also will now be comfortable to return and travel Europe in depth, if they have the opportunity.

The decision to teach at Buena Vista was one of the best decisions of Mac's life. When they moved to Storm Lake and he started teaching, he thought he would probably be there just a couple of years before moving on to another school, but 30 years later, he was still there.

Buena Vista afforded so many opportunities. Mac was able to grow there, be an important part of the college community, and get to know all the students and be a major influence on their lives. He was able to grow professionally in a way that he would not have been able to do in a place with an enormous number of artists, all trying to claw their way to the top to be noticed. The school respected his work and let him be 'Mac'.

Early in his tenure at BV he was asked right away to give speeches at several important events, which scared Marie to death. The first time was at a major faculty and trustee dinner. Marie was so apprehensive, but the Dean had complete confidence in Mac and told her not to worry, he would be fine. Mac got up and gave a presentation about his work like a pro speaker, but in a very 'Mac' kind of way. It all went well and the audience seemed to enjoy the insight into his work. Mac was always so confident and never a bit nervous, which is amazing considering his background and no previous experience.

Mac started teaching for a yearly salary of eight thousand five hundred dollars in 1971. It was a pretty small amount, but seemed like a fortune since they had been married and on their own since their third year in college. But the school administration always gave him nice raises, top amount of merit raises, along with raising his salary by twenty percent twice in his tenure there. He felt he was well paid. On his beginning salary they bought a house, 'Bertha' his prized new International pickup truck, had their third child, and made vacationing and 'building memories' a priority.

At that stage in their lives they had to do everything on the 'cheap', but they never considered putting it off until they could afford to do it first class. In 1977, the family loaded up their big, three row seat, Chevy station wagon with all their camping equipment, chuck wagon box on the top of the car, and all five bikes, and headed south. They just meandered for five weeks. They looked like the Clampetts from the ' Beverly Hillbillies' going down the road, with bikes hanging off the car in all directions.

In contrast, during the 'energy saving time' of President Carter's reign, and doing their duty to the cause, they had switched from the gas-guzzling Chevy station wagon to a midsized Grand LeMans. One summer, leaving directly from the kid's conference swim meet, they proceeded to head out to the west coast to San Francisco for Mac's conference. At that time the kids were all grown and measured from to 5'9" to 6'5"' with Marie being the shortest. Needless to say they were all stuffed into that car and they drove and camped over all those miles in July, and the air-conditioning had stopped working in the car. They crossed the Great Salt Lake Desert and swam or floated in the lake. It was interesting but a forsaken part of the country. While going across the desert, they saw no hint of animal life, except for a bird, which they hit with the car. Mac said he was sure the bird had committed suicide.

They saw about everything one could see on this trip. They marveled at the landscape of Montana, traveled down California's Highway 1, went to Carmel , and swam at Big Sur, camped under the redwoods, and saw Yosemite National Park. During the day, while they were in San Francisco and Mac was at his conference, the family would sightsee, and Mac would join them in the evenings. It was a great trip. On the way home they camped at Lake Tahoe and picked up a couple enormous pinecones which they had to store behind their heads, because that was the last inch of room left in the car.

When the kids were all grown and out of college, Mac and Marie bought a large fifth wheel camper to travel in. The kids wondered why they didn't have that when they were growing up and vacationing! Hum, maybe the words, kids growing up and college, might be the reason, but at the time no one complained and they just enjoyed the experiences and were thankful for the memories.

Two summers, when the kids were in grade school, the family went on RAGBAI, which is a bike ride across Iowa, put on by the Des Moines Register. It is a yearly event that last six days and goes from the Missouri River on the west side of Iowa, to the Mississippi River on the east side. There is a designated route, which is different every year, and over 10,000 bikers are on the ride. The riders must stay in the designated town on the route each night, which provides plenty of food and entertainment, and there are also plenty of non-profit organizations everywhere on the ride selling food. The ride covers sixty-five to one hundred miles each day, with solid bikers on the designated roads. It is a blast and incredible feat for everyone of all ages. You are riding along the countryside talking to fellow cyclists, and you think you have eaten so much you are stuffed, but then a stand selling homemade pie and watermelon comes along and your handlebars just turn that way. The family would ride every mile across Iowa and come home gaining weight. They rode both years with regular, plain, FreeSpirit bikes from Sears, without any problems.

RAGBRAI (Registers Annual Great Bike Ride Across Iowa) just reached Burlington, IA overlooking Mississippi River- last day, 455 miles behind us.
Youngest daughter, Marcy, stayed home this year.

Free beer at Morning Sun Fire Department. ( Mac, Med, and a pharmacist that we met on the ride) The men drank many beers here and at the golf course in the next town, so arrived at camp very happy.

    Another year, when the kids were in grade school, the Horneckers went with friends to the Boundary Waters in Minnesota.  As a side note, they were the family of the girl Marie recognized coming home on the bus their first year in Kansas City.  The Boundary Waters are millions of acres of lakes and islands that connect with only small portages at times.  There are no motorized boats, residences, or commercial properties allowed, so it is pure beautiful wilderness.  You take in what you will need and bring out what you have left.  There are designated camp sites to choose from and you need a permit to enter, so only a limited number of people are in the different areas.  Because of that arrangment you hardly ever see another human.

It is so peaceful and quiet except for moose swimming and crashing up the banks, and the loons. The kids thought it was their favorite vacation, and added more great memories.

Mac is getting his fishing pole loaded and ready to head out for 6 days with 4 adults, 5 kids, in 4 canoes, and enough dried and nonperishable food for **12 days**.

Had to hang bags at campsites so the bears would not get your food, and leave tents open if you leave, so bears go in and not tear up your tent. Melissa was concerned that the bears would poop in her tent. Mac assured her, if they found bear poop in her tent they would all be out of there

Storm Lake was a wonderful place to live, and especially in those days, a wonderful place to raise children. It was a beautiful lake, and the size of the town was perfect. Mac and Marie had such great friends and couples; that they vacationed with, spent holidays together with their children, which were close in age, and provided such a fun social life.

Mac had gotten his Iowa friends acquainted with his Missouri friends; who would all get together twice a year to pheasant hunt on opening day in Iowa, and to fish in the spring in Missouri, complete with a traveling trophy. Of course the girls would plan a weekend getaway to some hot shopping spot during these fishing/hunting times. This has been a tradition for over 30 years.

At Storm Lake
The race is on!
Racing with friends.
Mac is in farthest
sailboat with
multi-colored sail

Storm Lake was also great for winter sports like snowmobiling or skating, but close enough to Minnesota to ski at several good downhill skiing resorts. This was always a fun weekend activity for Mac's and other families. Of course the summer was the best time, and the lake was the center of activity. The lake is only three thousand acres, so anyone on the lake could be seen by all. If your sailboat turned over and you couldn't get it back up, someone with one of the hundreds of huge free standing telescopes (first thing to get when moving on the lake) would see you and come to your rescue. It was a big sailboat lake, and the sailboat club would have official races during the summer for everyone to enjoy. It was a beautiful site to see with all the colored sails.

There is a paved walking/biking path around half of the lake, and the rest can be ridden on a road. On one end of the lake, where Mac and his family lived, the waterfront and bottom were sand, with great beaches for the kids to swim and congregate. But the best factor of Storm Lake was the college, which added so much to the community. It was a great town and Mac and his family had such a 'rich' life during the years they lived there.

**Copper Mountain /Breckenridge**
**Hornecker Family - Marcy, Mac, Marie, Med, and Melissa**
'No guts, no glory' was Mac's kids motto, but Mac was a 'Bunny Hill' kind of guy, and when he took the wrong turn and ended up on a 'BLACK' trail, he was not embarrassed to ride on his butt, all the way to the bottom

Mac planned his retirement about five years before he retired. A year before his final days, he organized a thirty year reunion of all their former art students. He had the students send a piece of art for a composite art show which needed all the gallery spaces around town and the university. It was so rewarding to see how many of the former students were still producing art. They all got together and had several parties, but one night those that wanted, got up and made presentations of their art work. The reunion was the reward of 30 years of teaching for both of them.

Dennis Dykema, former student, and Mac
The perfect odd couple that taught together for 30 years

In October of Mac's last year, Dennis decided to also retire at the end of the school year. Now, there was a real serious push to replace both Mac and Dennis, and retain the progress and importance of the department that they had built.

After an extensive search, they made the decision to hire two outstanding former BV art students. Although Mac usually did not believe in 'inbreeding', he was in favor of hiring these impressive former students, and it turned out to be a good decision. Both of the candidates that were chosen continued on, knowing the strong teaching attributes of Mac and Dennis, plus good ideas of their own. The department continued on without a bleep, and even got better. Their own work was outstanding and set a good example for the students. Their classes grew and were full with waiting lists. In a few short years the university, after building a new Science Center, remodeled and added on to the older Science Center. They made the first floor and the new addition into an amazing new Art Department that would be the envy of any school. The university had been promising a new art department for years, and it was sad that Mac and Dennis couldn't have been there to enjoy it. But, they felt without them laying the ground work and establishing such a successful and highly respected art program, it would not have happened.

Mac and Marie had decided to retire five years in advance of the May 2001 date, when Mac would be 58. They wanted to move to a warmer climate, and the school offered a buyout that could not be passed up. They were from southern Missouri and knew that area still had hard winters. They would have to go farther south but did not want to go to the lower south. At that time the "snow birds", as the people in the north who winter in the south are called, were going to the far south to areas like Brownsville, Texas, or southwest to Sun City, Arizona. Mac and Marie thought that southwest Arkansas or northeast Texas would be just right. They also wanted to move to a real neighborhood, and not a retirement area, and somewhere that had trees and was green, opposed to the southwest. They also knew they wanted to move by a lake, since they had been only a block off Storm Lake for 30 years, and they knew they wanted to be in a university town because of the enrichment to the lifestyle.

Marie got on the computer and entered 'southwest Arkansas, northeast Texas, lakes', and all the lakes came up with the surrounding towns. After clicking on the towns, a place to contact their Chamber of Commerce would come up, and with a click, a city packet would be sent. During the January break, Mac and Marie got in the car and spent a couple of weeks looking at all the towns. They went to Arkadelphia, Arkansas first. They had thought of building on a lake, and Arkadelphia was just five miles away from a big lake called DeGray Lake. They took a scenic route going down to southern Arkansas to DeGray Lake, which was beautiful, but on a road that you met yourself 'coming and going'. The northwest half of Arkansas is in the Boston Mountains, and the rest of west Arkansas is in the Ouachita Mountains. Both mountain ranges are breathtaking, and a reason the state is called 'The Natural State". They stopped at a restaurant along the scenic mountain road, and the waitress said "whatsuallwant". Mac and Marie looked at each other and smiled; they knew they were in the south.

They got to DeGray Lake and quickly noticed that there were no houses around the shore. It turned out to be a Corps of Engineers dammed lake, and houses were not allowed to be built within one-half mile of the water. They later discovered, that because of this rule, the lake had almost zero pollution, was crystal clear, and you could clearly see down 30 feet. It was also a beautiful lake, of islands and coves, 29 miles long, and over 130 feet deep. Mac and Marie decided if you had to build that far away from the water, you might as well be in town.

They then went to downtown Arkadelphia and everyone was out walking around, and said, "Hi" and "Isn't it a nice day?, just so friendly. When they left Iowa, it was minus twenty degrees with several feet of snow on the ground, and the lake was frozen over about three feet deep. In Arkadelphia, that day in January, it was seventy-four degrees. Mac and Marie thought they had died and gone to heaven. Of course that was almost 20 degrees warmer that the normal temperature for Arkadelphia in January, but even the normal fifties would have been wonderful. Also there were winter flowers and some fruit trees blooming everywhere. They stopped at a restaurant that they immediately noticed was run by the local adult group home for mentally and physically challenged adults. The clients of the Group Home were doing all the jobs they could do, including waiting on customers and delivering the food. To Mac and Marie's surprise, the restaurant was full and being patronized by everyone in town. In contrast, there had been a huge controversy in Storm Lake, when the schools wanted to partially mainstream the local school age Group Home, and also have the disabled kids eat with the other students. Mac and Marie felt that a town that could embrace and support this activity said a lot about the town.

Mac and Marie also were impressed by the canoeing river that circled the town with canoe outfitters; that the city was about the same size as Storm Lake and also the county sea; with rolling foothills, and tremendously tall green trees; and both a state and a private university. They visited many other locations but went back home to Iowa with the decision that Arkadelphia, Arkansas was where they were going to land.

Mac and Marie had been asked so many times how they found and decided on Arkadelphia. The Chamber packet was wonderful, but Arkadelphia also seemed like a logical way to satisfy all their wants. In August 1997 they returned to Arkadelphia and bought a lot, planning to build their home in four years in 2001. It was a wooded lot of several acres, outside of the town, and on a dead-end street bordering a golf course. They always marveled at the good fortune to find this lot, and always thought it was the best location in the area, complete with fabulous neighbors.

In the summer of 2000, the Storm Lake newspaper printed a half page story about Mac retiring the following May. It wasn't soon before people started inquiring about buying Mac and Marie's house, which wasn't grand but was unique. They ended up selling it in November, without a realtor, but the buyers wanted possession the first of January. Of course they would sell it on those terms, so they scrambled to turn the heated and air-conditioned space of Mac's studio into an apartment to live in for their last few months in Iowa. It worked great, with a kitchenette, a new bumped out room for a bedroom, full bathroom, and a loft to store the enormous amount of stuff from the house, and still had room in the studio for Mac's work.

During this time in 2000, knowing Mac was going to retire, Buena Vista University commissioned him to do a large sculpture for the school that was financially provided by the former president. It was called Plato, of welded steel and ferroconcrete, measured 12' x 10' x 8,' and painted one of Mac's signature colors of dark blue-black.

**PLATO** 2001
steel and ferroconcrete
12' x 10' x 20
Buena Vista University   Storm Lake, Iowa

In 2000, Mac also entered the prestigious, competitive International Sculpture Exhibition on Navy Pier in Chicago for the spring and summer of 2001. The piece was accepted and needed to be built and installed while Mac was in the midst of retiring, organizing the reunion and art show for 30 years of art student alumni, building the commissioned sculpture for the University, building the garage in Arkansas to move into in June, selling the house, and moving everything that they had accumulated over 30 years out of the house.

**PRAIRIE FAULT**  2001
steel and ferroconcrete
9' x 16' x 8'
Pier Walk 2001
International Sculpture Show
Navy Pier, Chicago, IL
Presently at Northlake, IL

Before Mac and Dennis were officially finished at Buena Vista, they had to go through graduation. This year they both were asked to be the graduation speakers, and both were honored by the university, bestowing them with an Honorary Doctor of Fine Arts degrees, and both welcomed into the prestigious group of Professors Emeriti.

When it came time for their commencement addresses, they finished their tenure as always, and in true form. Dennis gave a wonderful speech with all the important words of wisdom for the future, and Mac told a 'Mac Story' with a point at the end. For those who actually listened to the speeches, they were probably amazed. After the graduation ceremony, one of the female professors walked up to Mac and told him, "That was one Commencement Speech and probably the only Commencement Speech that I will never forgot and I loved it." Most people probably were not listening, until all of a sudden they started hearing an unusual narrative, and it was too late to catch up and understand what in the heck he was talking about.

The speech was based on a 'Mac Story' about Horseshoe George.

## Horseshoe George

He was the first professional athlete from our community. Almost fifty years later and people still talk about him once in a while. When his name comes up, the stories from the old timers, the ones that knew him, really start to flow.

George was his name. No one knows what his last name was 'cause it didn't matter in those days. But everyone called him Horseshoe George. Ya see, George made his living being a horse. He would go from town to town doing rodeos. His game was bucking. He would take on all comers for a ten dollar bet, "Bet ya can't ride me for a minute" was his line. He was damn good! Nobody every rode George.

George was striking as a horse. He had a saddle that he custom fit for his short stocky body and even a bridle that he put in his mouth. He had short legs and wore bib overalls with the crotch almost to his knees, which made his legs look even shorter. With his bridle and saddle and on all fours, he would start to look like a horse. But the kicker was the horseshoes he had nailed to the soles of his plow shoes.

After the bets were made, the crowd would form an arena. George with the saddle, bridle, and horseshoes would start the transformation into the damnedest horse you ever saw. Nickering, snorting, pawing the ground, throwing clods with his shoes, he – was – ready. It never took a minute.

He might take on ten or twelve fools a day and it began to wear on old George. It made it a lot harder to get home at the end of the day before chores. He had some chickens to feed and had to bake some cornbread for his dogs and himself. He always had a lot of stuff that he took along, a wagon full that he pulled with a custom made harness. Things like his saddle and bridle, an ax, and a bunch of tradable items. He kept some fighting cocks tethered to the side of the wagon, those red ones with the long bright red tail feathers, because, everyone fought cocks in those days. There was always three or four of those old yellow cur dogs that followed him everywhere.

It was one of those hot, breathless days of August when George was on his way home. The roosters were panting and had their wings out to their sides as they squatted on the side boards if the wagon. The old dogs were just trotting in a line with their heads down, tongues out at full length, and sucking in that last drip of water, with a big gulp, just before it dropped.

He took a rest on the bridge in the shade of a big tree. Those cur dogs were down in the creek sprawled out in the water and holding their heads straight up with those big tongues hanging out of the side of their mouths almost down to their feet.

Right after the bridge was a big hill. Things were going alright 'til about half way up when old George balked. You could hear him nicker for a mile, 'cause there wasn't any wind. Then you could hear George the man cuss and yell "giddy up, you bastard"! George the horse would just snort and paw, but he wasn't going up that hill. Those damned dogs just went over and laid in the shade. Then George lost his cool. He unharnessed the horse, went around to the back of the wagon, got out his ax, went to the road ditch, and cut himself a tall sapling. He took some time to cut off the limbs, skin back the bark, and put his ax back in the wagon. He got old George back in the harness, yelled, "getup George'" and took the switch to himself. Damn! What a commotion! Yelling, whipping, cussing, nickering, and the sound of horseshoes on the rocks. In a few minutes they were at the top and things got quiet and the cur dogs were trotting alongside the wagon as usual.

Ya know, down by the creek on the bluff, where George lived in a cave with a lean-to, you can still see marks that his horseshoes made on the rocks.

This was the ending to his Commencements Address:

**So was George crazy? Some say crazy as a pet coon, OR WAS HE JUST DOING WHAT HAD TO BE DONE?**

By this time all of Mac and Marie's kids had gone to college and were out pursuing their careers and families in many parts of the world.

Med graduated from Iowa State University with a degree in Technical Theater and Set Design and met a talented mezzo-soprano while he was technical director of the Des Moines Opera. They were married and had just returned from Hamburg, Germany where she sang in Phantom Of The Opera for three years. They were now living in her hometown of Duxbury, MA , on Plymouth Bay, and a mere twenty-eight hours away from Arkadelphia.

Melissa graduated from the University of Oklahoma with a degree in Meteorology (one of those storm chasers) and started dating her TA , who was getting his masters in Meteorology, and they were married. She also got a degree in math and computer science. They both got jobs in the Washington DC area until Melissa got an offer from University of Oklahoma to come back for a research project while she obtained a degree relating to Hydrology. Her husband, who worked for a weather related company and the National Weather Service in DC, was invited to return to Norman to work at NOAA's National Forecasting Center, continuing to improve on his computer tornado forecasting model, and obtain his PhD in Meteorology. While they were in Norman they had 2 boys, Andrew and Maclain, about three years apart. Since they were living in Norman, Oklahoma, it would only be about five and a half hours to Arkadelphia. Close enough to even go to the grandson's three and four year old basketball games.

Marcy went to Buena Vista University in Storm Lake for her first two years in Art, so her principal professors were Mac and Dennis. It actually was a wonderful time for both Mac and Marcy, although most thought he was harder on her than the other students. She lived on campus and had a great college experience. After two years Mac and Marie insisted she finish at another school, thinking it would be good for her to experience different professors and a different school than the one she had grown up around. There was a tuition exchange between Buena Vista and about 200 other private schools. She chose Drury University in Springfield, Missouri. It had several art history professors and was a very good school, although it didn't have the comraderie between students like Buena Vista. Marcy graduated with a degree in Art History and Photography. After working for a photographer in Springfield, Missouri, she started working in retail framing and now owns her own custom framing business. Marcy would now be 13 hours from Arkadelphia.

People continually ask Mac and Marie if they moved to Arkadelphia to be close to family. The answer is always, "no, because the kid's lives change, or they just up and move on you. But, you do need to be retired to have time for the long trips to visit them." Their motto for the kids was, "We don't care where you live just so it is a fun place to visit." They always felt that one of the most important jobs a parent has is to teach their children to be individuals and independent. At times, it was hard if the kids didn't fit into the local mold. They did always want to go their own way, and had the confidence to explore many unusual avenues. Also, they did live in many interesting places to visit.

Their son Med, was having strange symptoms just as he and his wife were leaving Germany and coming back to the states. The health care in Germany was fabulous, and because of the arm pain and his family history, Med had a complete heart workup just before he left. He would have a split second ' brown out' and then his left hand would close up and he couldn't open it. After a few months in the states, in February of 2000, he went to a doctor about a respiratory problem and mentioned the strange symptoms which were happening less frequently. The doctor ordered a brain scan and found a mass the size of a lemon. Med was lucky and got in to see the leading brain surgeon in Boston. Med underwent a six hour surgery with the top of his head cut open without anything for pain, so he could be alert and talk to the surgeon. This all took place in a sophisticated MRT machine, from Germany. The surgeon was inside the machine with Med, which took MRIs all during the surgery. Those MRIs were read by another surgeon, who would tell Med's surgeon where to cut, in areas he could not see. It was state of the art, but one-third of the tumor was growing into the brain, and when they tried to remove it, Med's foot dropped, so they stopped.

The tumor turned out to be the size of a large orange. It had grown for years so slowly that the brain had adapted to it without any discernible symptoms. It was an astrocytoma, which grows back 100 percent of the time, with little fine 'roots' growing out into the brain, making it is impossible to remove it completely. At the time Mac and Marie moved to Arkansas, the tumor was still growing as a Stage 1 cancer, so the doctors told Med it was benign. In the immediate family, only Marie knew that Med's lifetime was severely limited.

# Eight

## Arkadelphia, Arkansas
## September 11, 2001

Mac had always wanted to design and build his own house. One day, on a large dry erase board on the wall of the Storm Lake studio, he drew the picture of the house he wanted to build, and that was the only 'blueprint' or picture he ever drew. He did make a basic exterior foam core maquette to make sure the roof lines would come together correctly, but that was all.

During the January break in 2001, Mac and Marie went down to Arkansas and started building a three bay garage which consisted of a two car garage, and one bay for a small working studio. They finished it up in June of 2001 and made the final move of their belongings on the day of 9-11.

They had gone down to Arkadelphia on Mac's spring break to pour the concrete floor for the garage, but went home without it being done because of a '100 year' twelve inch snow that paralyzed everything. It hovered around freezing for days, so did not melt immediately as usual. The Interstate (I-30) which runs along the side of Arkadelphia, was at a standstill for several days, with all four lanes bumper to bumper of abandoned cars and trucks, minus those in the ditches. It was snow that came straight down, instead of sideways, as in Storm Lake, and the temperature, was only at freezing, so Mac and Marie thought it was warm and beautiful. As a couple of northerners, it seemed just crazy, and no one knew how to drive. They drove all over town with just their front wheel drive minivan, and stopped many times to help big four wheel drive SUVs get going again.

Arkansas house property- the driveway down to the area for the garage and house cleared of the virgin forest

Started building house **September 2001**

Picture taken **December 2002** (complete with sculpture)

They turned the three bay garage into a nice apartment; using one bay that would eventually become a studio, as a large kitchen and full bathroom with a clothes washer; put a wall between the two car bays for the middle bay to be a living room; and back of that bay walled off a bedroom area. They installed carpet, paintings on the walls, kitchenette, a new large refrigerator and apartment stove, and a small amount of concrete, of the future driveway, outside for a patio. This was home for the next fifteen months while they built the house.

So they were now in an apartment again, which reminded them of their early married life. They had so much company of friends, family, and past students during that time, who slept on a fold out couch in the living room. It was just fun.

It also gave them a nice place to live on site while they built the house. The two of them built every board, nail, and shingle of the house except; for hiring two carpenters for one and a half days to help set the forty-five foot beam for the great room, with the help of a crane; someone to dig the footings; a master electrician to do all the electrical work; and a rough in plumber. They also had the furnace and air-conditioning installed, and cabinets custom made, and friends that provided a lot of wonderful help. The house is a one level handicapped accessible ranch, 3,800 square feet, with a stucco exterior. It is on almost three acres of virgin forest, on a dead end street, surrounded by a golf course, and outside of the boundaries of town. This was their dream home designed and built by Mac. The only misgivings Mac had was that he wanted to build something exotic like a house cantilevered out over the ravine, but it had to be something the two of them could build. It turned out to be pretty unique, mainly because it was built with some unusual features and was like their own museum with large walls to showcase their art.

Marie landscaped the front yard with a pond system with three waterfalls, two ponds and a stream. She loved to garden in this new warm climate averaging forty-eight inches of rain a year, which was perfect for lush land and water landscaping. She went crazy.

Mac was the expert and Marie was the assistant/gofer. Mac layed out and prepared the footings to be dug, and the concrete was poured with the aid of a concrete pump truck. The footprint of the house was an odd configuration, but basically without counting the garage, was ninety feet by forty feet, on ground that had a twelve foot drop. Half way down the hill, the house turned at a twenty degree angle. Mac laid over twenty-five hundred concrete blocks, for the foundation around the perimeter, and the support pillars throughout the interior.

He refused to use a laser and laid all the foundation with a ninety-five cent string level. The foundation went all the way around, down the hill, around the kink and back up the hill, and met where he started, and he was less than three-fourths of an inch off.

Marie had found a great old large concrete mixer in Iowa, in a barn lot with a flat tire and surrounded by knee high grass. She paid fifty dollars for it, and it is still in full use today. Marie mixed all the concrete and got the concrete blocks to Mac as he laid the foundation and pillars.

The rest of the house went the same way. Mac would know what to do and just tell Marie how to do her part. They went all the way from hanging by their toenails, thirty feet off the ground nailing rafters to the roof of the great room, to mixing and pouring concrete for the back patio. They installed about one hundred fifty feet of windows, which were mostly floor to ceiling and were attached together as units.

The great room was twenty-four by forty feet with large trapezoid windows on the top of each end with solid windows and glass doors below. They just didn't have the muscle to put the large upper trapezoid windows in, so they asked at the lumberyard, where they had bought most of their materials, who they could get to help. They had become a legend at the lumberyard and there was always a fight within the yard workers, as to who was going to deliver and see the progress. The lumberyard suggested a local contractor who worked all over the state, including big houses in the mountains. When Mac and Marie called, they got him on his cell phone on his way back to town, and he swung by to look at the job. He said to have everything ready by the next morning and he would have a crew there to muscle the windows in. The next morning, his crew of eleven guys arrived, and after a couple of hours they had the windows installed. Marie got ready to write a check and ask the amount, and the contractor just shook her hand and said, "Welcome to Arkadelphia!" That was the common attitude that they found from everyone. Everyone came immediately when they were contacted, and they had fun all working together. Also everyone was very reasonable and fair, and the materials were much cheaper than they had expected.

In Storm Lake, Mac knew an architect who built a lot of churches with beautiful beams. He had been wondering where he would get the beam for the great room. The architect told him he got his beams from an outfit in Arkansas. It turned out to be just a little over an hour from where they were building.

Mac and Marie actually had a great time building the house. They would get up and eat breakfast but would not allow themselves to start working before 8:00 am; took a morning break; stopped for lunch at noon and ate and watched a little TV or took a nap; returned to work at 1:30pm; took an afternoon break; and quit at 5:00pm. They would only work five days per week, so it was like a very nice job. They watched a lot of HGTV. When they saw or read about a great idea, since they were the builders, they could make a changing decision, and thirty minutes later, the idea was built into the new configuration.

When the electrician and rough in plumber arrived, and asked to see the plans, Mac would point to his head. That was all there was and the electrician and plumber were all very accepting. At the end of the project, Mac and Marie needed to borrow money from the bank to finish the exterior. The bank wanted the blueprints, which Mac then had to draw up after the fact. The bank also made it clear that Mac and Marie should have borrowed the money from the beginning. Mac and Marie understood but were disheartened. They had been so proud of themselves to have accomplished so much without needing to hock themselves into debt for years. There was no pat on the back there.

The house was getting close to being ready to move into when Med's tumor had jumped to a higher level and he had to start chemo treatments. The holiday season was around the corner, so Mac and Marie started putting in longer hours. They desperately wanted the house ready to move into so they could have all their family together for Thanksgiving.  The carpet was layed and the furniture delivered just one day before the family arrived.  The official day of moving into the house was 15 months after they started building.  As Marie was sweeping the carpet after the layers had left, she stopped and looked around, and for the very first time was so amazed, and thought, "I can't believe we did this!"  So many people thought they were crazy and it would be an impossible job for the two of them.  Marie never let herself think of the probability of not being able to pull this off.  She just kept up the enthusiasm and had blind faith, but at that moment it hit her.

  Mac never gave it a second thought whether the house could be accomplished.  The house was not a piece of art, but Mac could not have been any prouder of his accomplishment.

  When Mac and Marie were looking at the lot, they noticed the closest house across the street had a sculpture in front.  When they returned after buying the lot, to start getting the ' lay of the land' and a place to plan a house, the neighbor came over.  He invited them to come over the next evening to visit, and to give them a list of subcontractors he used to build his house three years before.

  The county, and over half the counties in Arkansas, were 'dry', which means it was against the law to sell or serve anything containing alcohol.   Mac and Marie wanted to take something for the neighbors that night, but were afraid to take a bottle of wine, so they took a bouquet of flowers.  The first question out of their neighbor's mouth was, "what would you like to drink?", and he opened a cabinet full of liquor and two wine refrigerators.  To top that off, the house was full of original art.  This was the start of a wonderful relationship with great neighbors and dear friends.

  He also turned out to be the Vice President of Academic Affairs of Henderson State University in Arkadelphia.  His mother had been a professional artist, he was a professional percussionist, and his wife was a professional pianist, so they were very interested and supportive of the arts.  What luck!  He was also very interested in the art department, and the minute we moved he started trying to get Mac to agree to teach sculpture for the university.  After about a year of, "You're going to teach sculpture for us , aren't you," one day Mac returned a "Maybe in the spring" and the rest is history.  Unbeknownst to Mac, soon after they met and he saw pictures of some of Mac's work , he  told the Dean of the Art Department that he had a sculpture instructor for her.  The dean of the art department, was a funny, blunt, outspoken painter, and probably afraid of who was being pushed off on her.  When Mac went in to meet her, they immediately hit it off.  Mac really enjoyed her 'say it like it is' outspoken, rough cut personality.  She was a Hoot!

  Henderson State had great studio space with a foundry in a Butler building, which Mac had always wanted at the university in Storm Lake.  It had a BFA program, but had just picked up adjunct sculpture teachers for fifteen years.  The foundry hadn't been used in years, and most of the equipment and parts of the foundry had slowly disappeared.  Mac soon improvised to get the foundry up and working and filled the department with his own equipment, from sanders to plasma cutters to mig welders.  Mac taught Beginning and Advanced Sculpture and Advanced Independent Study.  From the very first day, they treated Mac like a 'rock star' artist.  They were so pleased to have him use the facility for his own commission work and let the students experience the total process and see what was possible.  The dean of the art department retired and was replaced with a spitfire, who was very organized, extremely appreciative of everyone's efforts, and again treated Mac like a rock star. One day at the beginning of the academic year, they had a pizza lunch meeting with the students and faculty. The Dean was introducing all the faculty to the new students, and when she got to Mac, she said, "If you want to have a life-changing experience, take a class from this guy, Mac Hornecker" and then all his former students jumped up and started clapping. Mac was smiling but was actually very moved.

Through Marlene at Olson Larsen Gallery, Mac had several large commissions after he retired and moved to Arkansas, and of course, after the house was mostly finished. One of the great advantages of being in Arkansas was the pleasant winter temperatures, which were perfect for working outdoors all winter.

In 2005 the MidAmerica Group, in Urbandale, Iowa commissioned Mac to do a sculpture that would be placed on a grassy island of the street, in a commercial corporate office park. This park also contained a Hilton Garden Inn. The space was large and needed a big piece . The sculpture was 'Hills, Field, Wind, and Rain' of Corten steel and ferroconcrete. The size was 15' x 62' x 26'. Corten is a special steel that forms a rusty deep orangey-red colored protective crust, which is not only beautiful but maintenance free. This piece took a semi, a 20 foot flatbed trailer, and a smaller trailer to transport it from Arkansas. Of course a crane had to be ordered and be there as the semi arrived.

The installation was quite a process, which Mac loved. The tense part of an installation is that everything has to be lined up perfectly. The footings consisted of a thick slab or slabs of concrete, with concrete pillars into the ground several feet deep. The elements would be lifted off the semi with the crane hopefully without scratches, dents, or breaks, and avoiding injuring anyone in the process. Mac would then go to work bolting all the elements together, removing the installation bolts, drilling in the concrete anchors into the footings, and on many other pieces, paint the last total coat of paint.

This sounds simple, but this is really just the big stuff to do. The little stuff is a list a mile long, like making sure they have a generator on site to run the drills and any electrical equipment needed, to knowing the size of openings in the buildings that the crew would have to muscle the heavy elements through.

When Mac made a piece, he would always set it up in the studio or studio parking lot for a trial run to check for problems. But it was amazing how the metal would never stay exactly the same after the long trip. When he would set it up at the installation location; to quote the DesMoines Register, "the Man of Steel"would always need to gentle prod or coax it into place, and the word coax is being used mildly. The unexpected problem usually stemmed from the variance in the floors of where it was made, and the trial setup, and the footings at the installation site. This was just the 'nature of the game'.

**HILLS, FIELDS, WIND, AND RAIN   2005**
Corten and ferroconcrete
15' x 22' x 26'
North Park Business Center
Urbandale, Iowa

   As Mac stated to the DesMoines Register, " The piece swoops up and out of the landscape and swoops back in like the Iowa Hills."  During his years in Iowa, his art was influenced by the surrounding landscape.  "My pieces have become more lyrical with curving lines.  I'm not reproducing the landscape, but using it as the essence".  ...Hornecker's piece was designed to be seen from the perspective of a passing car, and is installed with that view in mind.  "There will also be a nice view of it from the interstate".  ....Hornecker handles the installation himself.  "I like the installation process... and getting the piece to the location is really the biggest challenge,"


 In the next few years, Mac had several major commissions, and of course, he was entering competitive shows and solo and group shows.   To do this, an artist must be constantly making art so he has current pieces to show.  Because of the good foundry setup at the university, Mac could make a lot of large pieces cast in bronze and aluminum.  These pieces were especially important for the gallery and museum shows, because they were a more manageable size.

And once again, Mac had his students casting shortly into the first semester of beginning sculpture. As mentioned before, this let the students know they were in a serious sculpture class. They may not have known it until later, but they were getting proficient at an area of sculpture that is taught in very few art departments. When his students would apply for graduate schools, or professor positions after getting their MFA, the casting and foundry experience would always separate them from the pack. Fortunately they did realize how lucky they were to study under Mac and treated him with respect and admiration and once again were thrilled with the little thumbs up gesture, or a "not bad!

**Trout Stream**
23" x 23" x 39"
Bronze
Allied Group

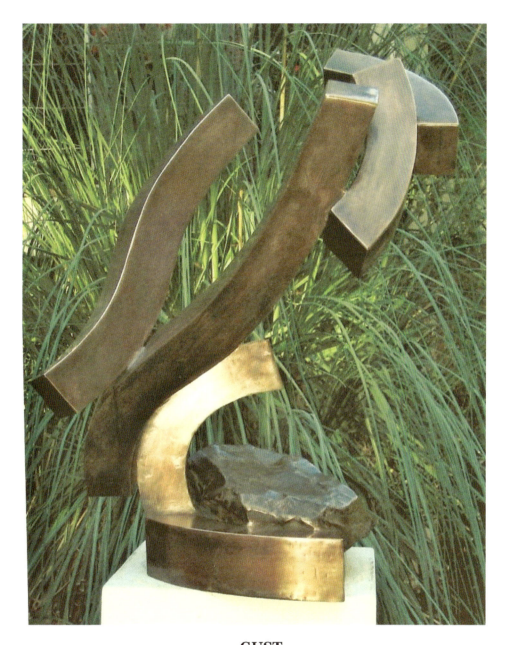

**GUST**
35" x 25" x 19"
Bronze
Allied Insurance

**MOUNTAIN BREEZE**
29" x 36" x 13"
Bronze

In 2006, Allied Insurance purchased several of Mac's Bronze pieces and commissioned him to make two more. They wanted a total of five sculptures, to give as gifts to all their corporate headquarters. 'Gust' and 'Trout Stream' were two of those sculptures that are pictured.

In 2007, Mac's Bronze sculpture called 'Mountain Spring' was accepted into the Delta Exhibition 2007. This is an annual six state juried show for all media, held at the Arkansas Art Center in Little Rock. 'Mountain Spring' was one of 66 pieces chosen from 596 entries, and was awarded the Delta Award.

**MOUNTAIN SPRING**
Bronze
20" x 43 " x 15"
private collector
Delta Award, Delta Exhibition 2007

**BABBLING BROOK**
Bronze
32"x 48" x 16"
Iowa State Bank
Urbandale, IA

**FALLING WATER**
2006
5' x 5' x 6'
Bronze
Iowa State Bank
Urbandale, Iowa

In 2006, Mac was fortunate to have two large commissions. One was for the new Iowa State Bank branch being built in Urbandale, IA, a suburb of DesMoines. The new branch had already acquired the Bronze piece called 'Babbling Brook'.

The commission was for a sculpture to be a wall piece, for the front of the large fireplace in the lobby. Mac got the dimensions from the architect and went home and constructed 'Falling Water". It was Bronze measuring 5' x 5' x 6' which was a combination of casting and welded Bronze, and was extremely heavy. Mac arrived in Urbandale at the Bank with people to help him install the piece, but it did not fit. The architect had changed the dimensions and lowered the ceiling without notifying Mac of the change. Mac and his crew, who traveled many miles, struggled to get the piece loaded up again, to take back to his studio in Arkansas. Back at the studio, he cut off part of the bottom and redesign the piece. When he arrived there to install it the second time, the strong construction crew was nice enough to help Mac muscle the big heavy piece into place. Of course it had to be anchored and bolted into the wall because of the amount of weight. This was further complicated with the brackets built into the piece and the change of dimensions. Things are never as simple as they seem. Falling Water is a beautiful piece, although not one of Mac's favorites. For most people, it is their favorite sculpture of all his work. All the changes probably took a lot of the 'love' out of that commission for Mac.

About this same time, the Ryan Company, and an architect who had always supported Mac's art, commissioned him to do a piece for the entrance of a new small shopping center called Marketplace Mall. The small mall is in Clive, Iowa, another suburb of DesMoines. The city of Clive was starting an initiative to have sculptures all over their city, and this was to be their first.

The piece was called 'Prairie Emergence" and made of welded steel and ferroconcrete. It was a tall piece, measuring 22 feet high. It is in a prominent location, on one of the most traveled main streets in the area. The piece also has flood lights on it at night, which make it really come to life.

**PRAIRIE EMERGENCE** 2006
steel and ferroconcrete   22' x 12' x 15'
Marketplace Mall   Clive, IA

Night View

In 2006, their son Med's brain tumor was growing and he was becoming more and more debilitated. He was a patient of the head of oncology at Dana Farber in Boston, so was getting the best care available. They had started him on a clinical trial of a drug that had been used before but Med took a different dosage schedule. It had worked far better than ever before and probably was responsible for giving him two to three better years.

During that time Med and his wife had a baby boy, and their only child. Med was a 'stay at home' Papa for the first two years, until he started having frequent seizures. From the very first day that they found the tumor, Med was the one who was always trying to keep everyone from worrying. He never asked for help or complained. In 2006 and 2007 Mac and Marie took their fifth wheel trailer and stayed at a nice campground in Plymouth, just 7 miles from Med's home in Duxbury, Massachusetts. When the day came that Med could not be left alone, they would go to Med's house when his wife Beth, would leave for work, and went back to the trailer after supper. It gave Med's family some family time alone. Until Med's condition progressed, Marie would stay and help while Mac would return to teach his class. During the cold November of 2006 they were needed, but the campground had already closed for the winter. A wonderful neighbor who lived across the driveway, had an unused apartment in her home, which was a remodeled cranberry warehouse, and was so kind to let Marie stay there. But as time went on, Med needed help full time for him to be able to stay at home. He finally lost the fight on October 22, 2007, just ten days after his son's 4th birthday.

Once again they were reminded that life can be so short. He was 39 years old. All their loses in life were so tragic, but nothing is as bad as losing a child.

Mac and Marie returned home to Arkansas with incredible support from all their friends who made it their job to keep them busy. Mac turned to his sculpture and immersed himself in his work. Looking back, it is amazing how much he produced. If he wasn't working on a commission, he made medium size pieces and many maquettes, just anything to keep busy.

Three days after Med died, Mac was notified he had been chosen for a large commission piece to be installed in the park along the levy in Clinton, Iowa. This was such a blessing for Mac, certainly professionally, but mostly mentally. The piece, 'Rivers Edge' was installed in May of 2008. It was painted steel and ferroconcrete and measured 12' x 28' x 15'. It was in a wonderful location just over the levy from the Mississippi River. The town had built many types of activities and entertainment facilities along this levy, so it was a great place of enjoyment for the town and visitors. Mac's sculpture was located next to a big landscaped water fountain park, along with a swimming pool, ice skating rink, outdoor theater, semipro baseball field, new camping park, playground, and even grounds with proper hookups for vendors and craft events. Of course the big draw was the Riverboat, with shows and the Casino. Someone in that old river town had a vision and backed it up with results.

**RIVER'S EDGE** 2008
painted steel and ferroconcrete
12' x 28' x 22'
City of Clinton, Iowa

**HURRICANE** 2009
painted steel and
ferroconcrete
9' x 7' x 6'

**PRAIRIE BREEZE 2008**
steel and ferroconcrete
6' x 9' x 6'

**SPRING FLOWER**     2008
painted steel and ferroconcrete
6' x 6' x 6'
Bernice Garden, Little Rock, AR

**MOUNTAIN DRAFT**
welded steel
7' x 7' x 3'

In 2010 Mac decided to take off the fall semester but continue with teaching the spring semester. The school, as always, was very accommodating and understanding. Mac and Marie had been so many places, but had never seen much of the northwest and the southwest. They decided to leave the first week of May and meander out west. It was a wonderful trip, without a plan or schedule or any reservations, except for one. If they saw something interesting, they would stop and stay as long as they wanted. They started out through the panhandle of Oklahoma and meandered all the way up to Seattle. With old Storm Lake friends, now living in Eugene, Oregon, they hopped on a cruise to Alaska. That was their one reservation. Just a few days before the trip, the cruise line called and asked if they and their friends wanted to each be upgraded to a penthouse suite. What a special trip that was. Alaska was the last thing on Mac's bucket list, so what a way to see Alaska.

After circling back home by way of the northwest, they touched base at home, and then took out for the east coast. They picked up two of their grandsons, now in Indiana, and then on for their annual camping trip to Plymouth. There they joined their other grandson in Duxbury, Massachusetts, by Plymouth, for several weeks of camping. After flying the two Indiana grandsons back home for their school to start, Mac and Marie headed out to meander up the coast of Maine, and finally headed for home in September - a total of seventeen thousand miles. What memories!

The year went on as usual, with a cruise in the spring with old Missouri friends and then their annual trip to Plymouth, Massachusetts to camp with Med's son and visit Med's family and friends again. They had gotten used to being at the campground in Plymouth when Med was ill, and after that, they discovered that in July and August, Arkansas was a hot place to be. The average temperature in Plymouth was usually about 85 degrees instead of 100 or more degrees at home.

They came back in the middle of August so Mac could finish a piece he wanted to enter in the Delta Show, as the entry was due in September. Mac did finish the piece and submitted the pictures for his entry just in time.

He also wanted to submit an application for a major commission for the Sioux City Art Center, for a piece to be put on their front lawn. The end of September, he was notified he was one of three finalists to submit proposals for that commission.

He started immediately with the ideas rolling. The day of October 10$^{th}$, he got up early and drove to Hot Springs to get aluminum to make a maquette for the commission proposal, and then went on to Little Rock to pick up supplies for his next semester class. He returned home about noon and then headed to the studio and started working on the wood model and the final maquette. He was so happy and he was on a roll. He came home about suppertime and sat in the swing with Marie and told her all about his idea for the commission even down to the footings he was going to use. He was so sure he had a great chance to get this commission. The Sioux City Art Center had always been special to him. Several of his students had gotten jobs there and worked there for internships, and he was their first show in their new facility.

After supper they were watching TV and Mac started having strange abdominal pains, and twenty minutes later he was gone.

It was such a shock to everyone, including his doctors. Mac felt like he was in the best physical shape he had been in years, and 2 weeks before, he had topped out an echo stress test at the cardiologist without even getting winded, and had a complete physical with his doctor with perfect stats. The autopsy, which all was very questionable and most of the findings were known to be false, concluded there was a blood clot in his main coronary artery, so a heart attack.

The next day, word traveled through the art community around the country with lightning speed.
Early in the morning, the students went to the sculpture studio and built a big laminated wood wreath that they hung outside the studio. They also wanted to have their own memorial service at school. They found a great picture of Mac to put on the posters for the memorial service which turned out to be wonderful stories and tributes about Mac. The amazing thing is that he was only an adjunct teacher! Many people said that it was too bad he didn't know how the students felt about him, but he did. He knew how they felt, and he knew the ones that had been floundering and he turned around to became important in the art world and in life. And Mac knew the ones that were so grateful for how he had influenced their lives. That is the special thing about being a good teacher. The Dean that hired Mac at Buena Vista, because he thought he could relate to the country kids, knew exactly what he was doing. Mac had been in the student's place, not knowing if they were college material, or had any 'talent', or knowing which direction to travel. He had so many good fortunes that helped him along, but the good teachers who were mentors made him able to succeed. Mac hoped he was doing a little **"Pay Forward"**.

**WREATH**
As soon as the students heard Mac had died, they went right to the sculpture studio to make this tribute that they hung outside from his hoist (pieces of wood hang from the wreath with messages to Mac)

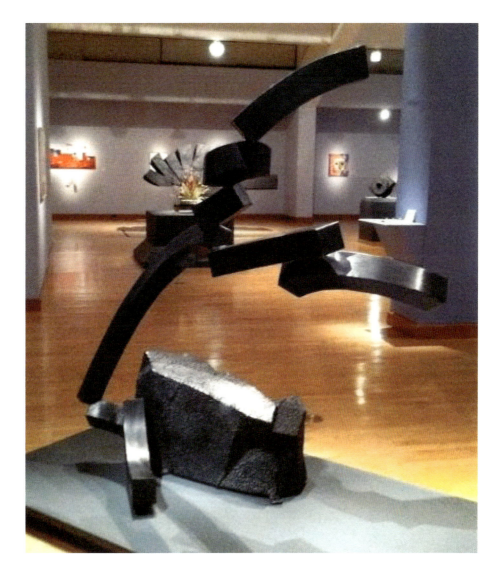

**Mac's Last Sculpture**
**PRAIRIE FLUSH** (Little Bird)
welded steel  6' x 7' x 4'
The family was notified two days after Mac's death that his piece was selected for
the 2012 Delta Exhibition.  It was one of 54 works selected out of 947 submitted

**FROM THE BRIDGE series   OUT BY NEWELL**
30" x 22"

**FROM THE BRIDGE series   #31 WEST**
30" X 22"

Drawing   30" x 22"

Drawing    22" x 30"

Mac always said he wished he had a nickel for every picture a photography student took of him grinding with the sparks flying. .

Sometimes they needed a little 'coaxing' !

photo by John Deason

Mac loved fabricating his sculptures

**STUDENT MEMORIAL POSTER**

Don't you know Mac would have loved the picture the students choose for their poster, but most important, <u>they knew</u> he would love it.

Unloading parts of sculpture off a semi flatbed truck
DesMoines Register:
**" I like the installation process.... And getting the piece to the location is really the biggest challenge"**

**PRAIRIE EMERGENCE Dedication Ceremony in Clive, Iowa**
Mac on right next to Marlene Olson
from Olson Larsen Gallery in West Des Moines
DesMoines Register / photo Warren Taylor

**MO BLUFF**  1977

2013 - Kids enjoying Mac's sculpture in his home town of Sheldon, Missouri

**A Happy Sculptor** photo by John Deason

**1976**

Photo from Hamilton Gallery, Inc, Des Moines, Iowa
Sculpture and Drawing show 1976

DesMoines Register

**1986**
Des Moines Register's November 1986 article title " **BIG MAC IS MAN OF STEEL IN ART WORLD**"

Mac taking his grandkids on another adventure
 left to right – Drew Baldwin
             Noah Hornecker
             Maclain Baldwin

**Family Portrait 2005**
left to right:
Back row: Beth, Noah, Med,
          Marcy Maclain,
          Mike, Melissa
Front row: Marie, Mac, Drew

# ADDITIONAL 'MAC STORIES'

## SWIMMING NAKED

Every afternoon in the summer we boys would go swimming. There were different places we liked to go like Doc's pond, the Baptizing Hole, or Slant Rock, and some other places with no names, just wherever the water was deep enough that we could try to drown each other.

Most of the time it was just boys, however, sometimes our parents and neighbors and girls went, so we had to wear suits. But the best was just us boys in the buff down at the creek. There were big grapevines that ran way up into the trees to swing on. We liked to get wet and go over to the sand bar and roll around until the only thing that wasn't covered with mud was the whites of our eyes. We invented Tarzan games. Mud Fight! Mud Fight! No one cared.

We would make plans the day before where we would swim the next day. We'd all show up on our bikes. Most of us had to ride at least a mile and sometimes three or four. We had those old flyer bikes with big tires. The road would get dry and sandy in the summer so it was pretty tough going most of the time. Most days were in the 90's and some were over 100 degrees outside. There was a smell to the creek that only those that have been here know. Cows liked to wade out and stand in the water and would have to be chased out, but in the excitement would leave behind floating pies. Usually by mid-June the skeeters got so bad we left the creek for farm ponds.

Like most boys, we spent a lot of time daring each other to do super human feats.

"Let's ride this tree down and use it to catapult someone into the water."

"Let's chase the cows out and race swimming the backstroke to see who hits the most cow floaters!"

"Let's ride our bikes naked as fast as we can to see who goes further out into the water."

It was the first of April-the first really warm day of spring – a Sunday. We were at this boy's house and several of our dads were there.

"You boys goin' swimmin' today?"

"Why when we was kids we always went swimming on St. Patrick's day."

We knew it was bullshit, but we would show those old farts. There we were, six teenage boys, stripped naked and lined up on the dock that we had built in the new farm pond.

"I'll go if you'll go."

"Well, I'll go if you go!"

"Ok, on three. One, Two, Three!"

KER-PLOP! HAAA!! Have you every felt every nerve end in your body scream?

We put on our clothes as fast as we could without drying off first. Socks on wet feet are always a problem. We must have reached about forty on those bikes going back to the house. We still brag, "We showed those old farts!"

Later that summer we went to try out a new pond. It was a great big one that was about a four-mile ride on the bikes. It was hot! None of us had on shirts, just underwear. Yes, we wore underwear in the hills, and jeans. Most of us were barefooted except for one kid that had lost a bike pedal and only had the bolt sticking out so he had on shoes. Otherwise, the bottom of his feet would be smoking by the time we got there. We had all stripped our bikes down, no fenders, grips, or any of that sissy stuff. Most of us wore shop caps to keep the sun out of our eyes. One guy had on sunglasses, the kind that highway patrolmen wear. He was cool!

We got to the pond and it was out in the middle of a pasture and there were no trees. The best thing, there were no blackberry briers or brush on the dam yet. There was a big rock right at the water's edge to get out on so we wouldn't get mud on our feet, which would get on our underwear.

We stripped down and bolted in. It was warm and clean, no cows. We basically were self-taught swimmers – dog paddle, side stroke, back stroke – just enough to keep from drowning and get to shore. We were dunking each other, having mud fights and having a wonderful time. We didn't even notice, but there was a car pulling up on the pond dam. She got out and it was the mother of one of the guys. She looked so big standing up there on the dam. All mothers looked big to us, for we knew we were in big trouble. She wore a flower print dress with big red roses and black high heel shoes with matching purse on her elbow. Her hair was back in a bun and her tortoise shell, horn-rimmed glasses magnified her eyes.

There we sit hunched down in the water. It's not proper to moon someone's mother, at least not in those days. We were waiting to hear the word.

She took off her glasses, purse, and high heels and got back and made a running start and made the best belly flop we had ever seen. There she was, dress and all. We learned what mud fighting was about from her. None of us had ever seen a woman swim. She said it was the first time in over twenty years. It was hard to say who had the best time. I think I still have mud in my ear where she nailed me.

The summers were a fun time of simple adventures, without all the frills of today's fancy and expensive toys and electronics.

## TENT MEETING

Every four or five years he would get the spirit and take to preachin'. These spells usually only lasted about six months or so, but he got the nickname of Saint Ives.

One time he hooked up with another preacher and had a big tent meeting back in the brush that lasted for a whole week. The other old boy had an old panel truck with two big cone-shaped speakers mounted on the top. They drove up and down the county roads calling people to the tent meetin'.

Saturday night was the big meeting. They had strewn some wire and light bulbs from tree to tree and stood concrete blocks on end and put 2x6's across them for seats. They had a tent put up in a pasture that seemed real big at the time. The panel truck was parked up front with the speakers and PA system ready to go. When they turned it all on, the lights gleamed.

The meeting started. Cars were parked all around the tent. People that didn't go, reported that it could be heard five miles away. What a meetin'- dancing, praying, singing, testimonies. Then the devil showed up in the form of a Hereford bull.

That bull attacked that panel truck. The tent cleared real fast. The meeting came to an abrupt end with Saint Ives using every cuss word in the book.

A week later the old bull was standing in the shade with the cows, chewing his cud as gentle as a lamb.
What was left of the tent and panel truck was down the road savin' souls in the next county.


## PORCH MULES

Their barn blew down so they had no place for the mules. Five males and none were under twenty years old. They were those 'ol black mules with brown noses. He had broken a leg while cutting wood and had neglected the mules for a while. Their manes weren't roached and were full of cockleburs as were their tails.

Anyway, these mules took to staying on the front porch of the house. When you drove up to most houses there might be four or five hounds, or even cur dogs on the porch, but this is the only one I ever saw with mules.

One night a guy had car trouble down the road. He was a stranger in our parts, but he saw a light and went awalking up to the house with his flashlight. He got one shine of the eyes of those mules as they jumped off the porch and came arunning up to the fence. He ran all the way to town. "Biggest, ugliest, damn dogs I ever saw".

He didn't get his car until the next day.

# FLUFF HAY

Old people can get real strange in their ways and most of all they get tight and afraid someone is going to get them.

This old couple didn't have much, just a couple of old horses and two or three old cows. They had quit farming except for a garden, but had kept the horses (they were too old to sell). The cows were old too, but they gave enough milk for some butter and most of the milk went to feed the cats. They had lots of cats as well as a big watchdog.

They had no kids. She had a sister that lived in another community that she had not seen in several years but they talked on the phone a lot, for hours. The old crank phones were about like two tin cans on a string anyway. They decided to go for a visit, for the sister was a feelin' puny.

They were going to be gone for four days. So they asked us to do their chores. People always did chores for other people while they were gone. That was mighty neighborly and no one expected to be paid, they could just help you out sometime. Chores couldn't be much there anyway – two horses, three cows, a dog and few cats.

So we went down for the directions. It was winter, so hay had to be fed to the cows and horses. We asked why they had the horses in the barn and not running loose in the pasture with the cows. They had been in the barn for about a year.

"If we turn them loose, we can't catch them," they replied.

The directions for the horses were a coffee can of oats a piece and two flakes of hay, fluffed up. The cows get a can of oats while they're milked in the stanchion. Then feed the milk to the dogs, mixed with corn chop and the rest to the cats. After the cows are milked, give the two flakes of hay (flake referred to about six inches of hay from a square bale) and fluff it up. We asked why to fluff the hay.

"It's not much hay so it makes them seem like they're getting more"!

We turned the horses loose for four days. The old nags ran and bucked and rolled in the dust. They were old but they ran with their heads and tails high with a grace of a young horse. They shared bales of hay with the cows. It was the first time they had been full in a long time.

That winter the old man died. She sold the farm, the horses, and the cows. The cats stayed and the dog moved with her to her sister's.

# OLD MAID AND BULL

There was on old maid that raised some good polled shorthorn cattle. They were real dark red with very few roans. The old maid kept pretty much to herself. You hardly ever would see her at a pie supper or something like that. She spent all her time babying her cattle. They were all like pets and would come right to her when she called their names.

Most people milked in a barn. Not her, she did it the old way – by just milked the cow where they stood. It took her a long time to do chores because she had to carry the milk clear back to the smokehouse. After all, she wasn't going anywhere. She didn't even have a car. All of her money was squirreled away somewhere, she never spent any.

My dad took a shining to her cattle. So, he stopped by to try to buy some of them. She wouldn't sell. He kept talking and tried to persuade her to sell him a young bull. Reluctantly, she agreed. She kept cows until they died of old age, but bulls she could get rid of.

We went to get the bull. These cattle never saw strangers so thy tended to take off for the back forty. Once in a while, they would stop and turn around, hold their head up high, snort, and take off again. Since we were coming, she had put a halter on the bull and had tied him to a cedar tree in the front yard. He was a good-looking, dark red yearling. We pulled in with a pickup with stock racks and all the cows took off. The bull was a little excited, but she calmed him right down by talking to him. He was easy to load.

As we drove off, the bull was bawling and the old maid stood by the road in her sewn bonnet, gum boots, and apron. She looked as though her eldest son was heading off to war.

We got the bull home and backed up to the barn and opened the tailgate. The side of the barn didn't even slow the bull down. It looked as though someone had driven a truck through it. It wasn't much of a barn anyway. That hole stayed in there until the day we tore it down.

We had to ship the bull off to the stockyards. He didn't pull a Lassie and head for home or anything like that, but showed no interest in our cows. My dad even had long talks with him, but it made no difference.

We decided that he was either heart broken or had not learned any social skills. Either way, he's bologna now.

# CUDDLES

Little ole ladies in the country always went to the mail box just before noon, right after they had dinner fixed but before they set down to eat. She had just picked up her mail and had stopped in the sunny breeze by the gate to see who was coming down the road. On the road ditch bank, the jonquils were in bloom and she had two or three in her left hand. She was right handed but there was a large bandage that covered most of that hand.

My Dad and I stopped to say howdy and had the usual "think it's gointa rain?" conversation. Dad noticed the right hand and ask, "What happened?" That set her off on a lambasting of the doctor. She said, "Any doctor that would do what he said was just no good."

She was a short old lady with a straw hat and apron. She had a little round face with little round glasses. Her house cat, Cuddles, was doing the weave around her legs. Cats were everywhere but Cuddles was the only one they let in the house. There must have been seventy-five or eighty cats at their place – barn cats. Some just headed for the weeds when strangers stopped. At night they had to milk one cow just to feed all the cats. That's the only time you could see all those damn cats as they lined up drinking from a trough by the side of the barn made of #2 2x6's nailed together with end boards.

Anyway, she had gone to the doctor to have her hand checked and had come away mad and was still mad as an old wet hen a week later.

The doctor looked at her hand. "How long ago did this happen?

"Three days ago."

"How did it happen"

"Well, I had Cuddles in the box with the tom cat and when I thought she had enough, I reached in to take her out, and she bit me."

"Did you put anything on the bite?"

"Turpentine."

"It would have done a damn site more good to put it on the cat!"

# IF IT WEREN'T FOR CHEWIN'

## Clive

The stories about him as the one that never got excited are legends. He never drove his old Chevy pickup more than 35 mph and he always turned his steering wheel holding his left hand stationary with his elbows resting on the window. He would make a loop with his thumb and index finger to thread the wheel through. With his right hand he would turn the wheel a few inches, and then clamp down with the left hand when he got a new grip with the right hand. After the corner, he would just let go and she would just straighten out by herself.

One hot day he had a wooden kitchen chair propped up on its back legs under a shade tree. He liked to read, so there he sat leaning back against that tree with his overalls, plow shoes, and straw hat, not the farmer kind but one of those 1950's Sunday go to meetin' kind. There was a nice breeze and he held the paper in both hands and had a can of snuff balanced on his leg.

The mailman stopped out on the road and yelled at him, "What ya doing'"?

"If…it…weren't…for…chewin'…nothin' ."

# LOAFING ON THE SQUARE

"Working harder than a cat covering shit on a marble slab" was his favorite expression, and he usually was, although about every three or four days of hard work it was time to loaf.

The county seat was a very good place to loaf, especially on Saturday. It seemed as though everybody for miles around liked to loaf on Saturday afternoon. The courthouse square was the best place. Some families got here early every week and parked their car almost always in the same place. Other people walked around the square, almost always counter clockwise, so the people in the parked cars could see them and howler at them. Of course, the young guys just drove around and around the square all afternoon a honking their horns and waving and yelling at everybody they wanted to impress. Then there were the 'parking meter hangers', men with both hands on top of the parking meter and leaning their chests on their hands. In any case, this was a major social event of each week. They talked and learned everybody's business as well as the business of people they didn't even know.

Some people went as they were and others dressed up. It seemed to be a time for social status. The way you looked and the way your car looked was very important. Some people would strut around when everyone knew they didn't have a pot to piss in. But on the other hand, everyone had a chance to impress the people from other small towns in the county, especially the teenagers and young adults. A lot of people got married to people from the other towns, so Saturdays prevented inbreeding that most people assume takes place in Missouri.

'Saturday loafing' was a fine art form to most of these people. The men had one liners for the kids. They knew you and your parents but couldn't resist saying things like "Who's that following you? or "Who's your shadow?". Kids were always acknowledged. Then, some people every week might say, "Here's a dime, go get an ice cream cone." Sometimes, we would get fresh roasted peanuts at the dime store. I can smell them now.

One of the best loafers had a parking meter on the west side of the square. He was always draped over it from about one till four every Saturday. He always wore blue overalls and blue work shirt with the top button always buttoned no matter how hot it was. Also, he usually wore the old style wool long handles, with the slit in the back, year round. His head was always topped with an old greasy felt hat with a big dark sweat stain that went about halfway up the side. Behind his ear was always a toothpick with another placed in the corner of his mouth. He chewed old twist tobacco that he kept in the left packet of his bib. A watch bob of brass with the likeness of Woodrow Wilson hung from the center hole in the overall bibs.

He would just hang there on his parking meter every Saturday talking to everybody and handing out dimes to the kids. He knew everybody because he was a well driller. Sometimes he had witched for a well using a peach branch and put on a good show for the customers. If people didn't believe in witching, he just drilled the well where they wanted. It made no difference to him. He always got water by either method. Retirement meant he could loaf and pass out his dimes. He might get a well drilling job for his son while he was there, but the joy of good water in the hole and a kid eating ice cream, he would say "life can't get much better".

# 'POSSUM

You've all seen days when the dust from the road just hangs there about three feet off the ground. It's hot and there is not a breath of air anywhere. Well, this was one of those days.

He hauled crushed rock, sometimes for people and sometimes for the county. He did alright, never had a new dump truck, but kept his clean, painted, and kept new mud flaps on her. He knew everyone and everyone knew him. He was never seen without a cigar butt in his mouth, never new, just half or less.

He had been hauling rock for a week on this road and this was the last day. He was like a horse headin' for the barn. The excitement was building and he was getting faster with each load so the dust was still hanging there when he would return. This was a strange road for all this rock, for there was only one person that lived on it and he didn't even have a car. He had gone up to his house to draw a drink of water from the well, and like to have never got away from the old man. But just the same, he would stop at the end of the day to see how the old man was getting' along.

The old man lived in a cellar about forty yards off the road. He had no family and nobody every stopped by, but that was ok. He gardened, fished, hunted, and ate a lot of greens and nuts and other stuff that he found in the woods. He did raise some chickens which he kept in the first room of his cellar. He lived in the back where there was just a table, a couple of chairs, a bed, and a stove. He would buy new overalls and wear them until they cracked at the knees, then buy some new ones, sometimes forgetting to tear of the tags. So, in his dresser he kept plates, fish hooks, rifle shells and things like that, all his stuff.

On his last load of rock, he looked toward the old man's place and saw a big cloud of black smoke. "Damn!" He slammed on the brakes and slid to a halt. Dust boiled in his face as he jumped out of the truck. He made a mad dash through the weeds to the old man's cellar, kicked in the door, and ran into a wall of excited chickens. He made it through the chickens and reached the door to the old man's room, kicked it in and was met by a wall of smoke, saw the old man on the bed, grabbed him and dragged him outside. He didn't see any flame, just smoke. The old man was sort of coming to, shook his head, looked around and said "I guess you shouldn't drink homemade Elderberry wine while youra bakin' possum!".

# TOBACCO SPIT

He was the best tobacco spitter around. Kids would gather around in amusement to watch him hit a June bug at ten feet. Skill is always appreciated no matter how useless.

Anyway, the neighbor lady up the road had this big old black dog, that long hired kind. He was a mean old bastard. He chased everybody that went past, especially us kids on our bikes.

One day the old man observed kids riding like hell to get by that damn dog. He yelled for them to come over, and they did.

"Let me have one of those bikes," he said.

Now this man was old and it amazed us that he could ride a bike. He didn't even have a car. Anyway, there he went, a bit wobbly at first, but by the time he got close to the old dog, he was doing pretty good.

Here came the old dog! He used the rapid fire technique. Three spits, one in each eye and the plug in the mouth.

Last time we saw the old dog that day, he was running his face through the grass like he'd been hit by a skunk. That afternoon, you could just see him lookin' out from under the porch.

Our hero had his moment of glory. Justice was served. Any skill has its place.

Now the kids are all grown. One of them told me the old man had died. When he was on his deathbed, this grown kid went to see him in the hospital. The old man had tubes and wires running to all the modern hospital menagerie. He said the old man was asleep and looked near death. The thought crossed his mind to slip a big chaw in the old man's lip. That's the way he would have wanted to go.

# AUTOMATIC TRANSMISSION

When people got old, they had trouble with their cars. It wasn't the car, it was them. You could hear them racing the engine and slipping the clutch. Once they lunged into the street a person could walk faster than most of them drove.

There was a grocery story on the corner of Main Street. The front had two windows and one door. The building was made of brick and built back in the 1800's. A wide sidewalk ran in front of all the stores on Main Street, and they all had sheet metal awnings that covered the sidewalk. The curb was high out front and cars parked diagonally.

On the side street there were no windows or sidewalk. This street was just gravel.
There was a bank of dirt that sloped up from the street to the building. Across the street was a 'garage/filling' station kind of place.

He had bought a new car. A 1953 Chevy Bel-Air with Power Glide. Here he came about five miles an hour with that Chevy six just a purrin', pulled into the side street, and put her in park. Oh, that sweet whine of the Power Glide. Then he strutted right into the store.

He paid for two plugs of Pick chewing tobacco and pranced back out to his car, got in and started her up. Then that sweet six started to roar and he dropped her into R. The race was across the street into the gas pump. He got her into drive and across the street to the grocery store, then back to the gas pump, then the store. After about the third time, the car jumped that slope of dirt and hit about three feet up on the side of the store.

The old man wasn't hurt. The guy in the store said that everything flew off the walls and went clean to the other side. "A good deal today on vanilla flavored corn flakes." He said.

# RUNAWAY HORSES

When people worked with horses, there was always a chance of a runaway. Anything could spook a team. There was always someone getting hurt.

Have you ever seen the old horse drawn mowing machine, the one with the five foot bar? There was some big prairie meadows still left that were hayed each summer. Blue stem prairie grass only got about a foot tall. It was said that it made such poor hay that it only kept the cows from eating each other. Anyway, this ole boy was mowing hay in this big meadow. There were six or seven teams a mowing. First, they would lay off a land, and then drive the horses around and around until that land was cut, which was just enough for the day. The sound of the sickle changed with each step of the team.

Bumble bees liked to nest in those meadows. They made their nest in the ground and protected them with great vigor. You guessed it; he mowed right through the nest. The horses were in a full gallop going out across the meadow. They cut a big figure-eight over about twenty acres and then headed for the creek. He was hanging on for dear life. It looked like he was a bouncing about five or six feet in the air when they disappeared into the brush. Everybody went running to see.

They found him lying in the weeds by the edge to the creek. The horses and what was left of the mowing machine were across the creek in the shade of a big walnut tree. As they came a running up, he rolled over and sat up.

"Hey, are you alright?"

"Yowl"

"What happened?"

"A bumble bee stung me on the top of the head, and it's still stinging!"

Another time in another place a man was cleaning out his chicken house. He had quite a few chickens and a pretty nice chicken house. Chicken houses always faced the south so as to use the sun in the wintertime. On the north side of the interior, he had built a roast out of two by two's that were hinged to the wall so it was easy to lift up and to clean under. There was chicken wire under the two by two's to catch any eggs that might slip out during the night. If you have ever run a scoop shovel through a rotten egg in a hot dusty chicken house, you know that was a good idea. But, there were always some that got through.

He had a nice team hooked to a manure spreader that he affectionately called the 'Turd Hearse'. Each load was hauled around the chicken house and spread on the field to the north. Chicken manure is real good fertilizer and he was going to plant corn there. It was a sunny spring day and he had about one load to go before he would be finished 'til next year. Rotten egg smell, manure smell, chicken dust and mites – it was a good thing that this was a once in a year job. He came back from the field empty and had just left the spreader in gear. The team was standing there about half asleep with their back foot balanced on the toe.

The spreader was almost full, just a couple more scoops. He was tired and had a big scoop full and hit the side of the spreader. The team took off like they were shot. Around the house and down the road they went at a full gallop. Chicken manure must have been going forty feet high. The road took on sort of a grey haze. Little feathers came floating to the ground and hanging up in the trees by the side of the road.

You could hear him cussing for about forty yards and laughing for the next mile and a half. As he went, he made little piles of manure spreader parts to pick up on the way back. It took most of the summer to get that thing put back together.

The weeds by the road sure did a little better that year.

# CAR / TRUCK

People used to go to town every Saturday. They bought groceries to cover things they didn't grow, loafed on the square, and most of all, went to the sale barn. Some went to the sale barn every week and also to every auction within twenty miles, but they never bought anything. It was their entertainment and social life. But most people would buy something once in a while.

Some people had so many kids they had to have a car. A pickup was okay in the summer but it was too cold for the kids to ride in the back in the winter.

You could get a calf in those days for two or three dollars. They were easy to get home in the trunk of a car. Most people kept gunny sacks in their trunk for such occasions. All you had to do was cut a hole for the head to stick out and tie him in. Bigger calves, however, were a problem.

I've seen people take the back seat out of the car and put it in the trunk so the calf could stand in the back with its head out of one window and its tail out the other. Those calves can get excited, which speeds up bodily functions. Sometimes they would jump into the front seat with the driver.

Also, we had a neighbor that used his car to haul his prize boar from farm to farm. The hog would just sit in the back seat and hang his head out the window. The hog always had a smile of anticipation on his face.

# ELECTRIC FENCE

Modernism was hard to understand by the old timers, especially electricity. They had trouble understanding how it worked.

This old boy had some old plow horses. He had pretty much quit farming except for a big garden. One of his horses was a fence rider. No matter how much grass there was, the old horse leaned against the fence until he rode it down. Then the cows and everything would get out. He thought an electric fence might be the answer to the problem.

One day the old man strung some wire, had it tied to those old porcelain insulators and hooked up to the juice. The next day, he called the vet out to look at his old horse. The old horse seemed to be in a daze and there was a big burn on his front leg.

"What in the hell happened"? ask the vet.

"He touched the electric fence, and it knocked him on his ass," the old man replied.

"What electric fence?"

"The one I made."

The man had used logic. 110 volts with a 100 watt bulb in the line left 10 volts for the electric fence.

One thing for sure – the old horse quit riding the fence

# RESUME

Mac Hornecker
106 Ridge Creek Point, Arkadelphia, AR  71923
Home   870-210-0706
horneckerm@gmail.com
**http:// machornecker.com**

---

Birth     April 10, 1943     Sheldon, Missouri
Died      October 10, 2011  Arkadelphia, Arkansas

**Degrees:**
　　MFA University of Oklahoma, 1970
　　BFA Kansas City Art Institute and School of Design, 1968
　　AA Joplin Junior College, 1964

**Permanent Public Collections:**
　　Kansas City, Missouri Parks System, 1967
　　Oklahoma Arts Center, Oklahoma City, 1970
　　* Oklahoma City Arts Council,  12'x12'x12', cast concrete,  'Untitled' 1970
　　Contemporary Arts Foundation, Oklahoma, 1971
　　Appalachian State University, North Carolina, 1976
　　University of South Dakota, 1977
　　City of Ames, Iowa, 19771979  'Prairie Bluff'
　　State of Iowa, Capital Complex 1977
　　*City of Sheldon Missouri, City Park,  9'x 8'x 52"  steel and stone , 'MO Bluff' 1978
　　** South Dakota Memorial Art Center, 16'x16"x32'  steel, stone, and stone ,  'Prairie Bluff'  1979
　　** Northwestern College, Iowa, 1980  'Aligned Landscape'   9'x10'x30'  Corten steel and concrete
　　 Buena Vista College, Iowa, 1982
　　**Bellevue College, Nebraska, 1984   'Mo River'   19'x19'x18'  Corten steel and stone
　　Pacesetter Corporation, Omaha, Nebraska, 1984
　　Bemis Co. Inc., Omaha, Nebraska, 1985
　　PaineWebber, Des Moines, 1988
　　University of South Dakota, Vermillion 1988
　　*Norwest Card Services, Des Moines 1989
　　Sioux City Art Center, Sioux City, Iowa 1989
　　Sheldon Memorial Art Gallery, Sculpture Garden, University of Nebraska 1989
　　* Iowa Farm Bureau Federation, West Des Moines 1989 'River'  10'x55'x10' welded steel
　　 MacNider Museum, Mason City, Iowa, 1992
　　Sioux City Art Center. Sioux City IA. 1995
　　** Employers Mutual Company, Des Moines, IA. 1996 'Prairie Wind'  15'x30'x10' welded steel
　　City of Omaha "Heartland of America Park" Donation 1996 'Pencil'   7'x7'x12' steel

*Hotel Pattee, Perry, IA., 1997 'Prairie Markers' 25'x60'x6' Ferro-concrete
*Pennsylvania College of Optometry, 1998 Philadelphia, PA 'Caution to the Wind' 34"x72"x32" Mahogany
The Suburban Fine Arts Center, 1999, 7' x3' x3', wood, Highland Park, IL
Northern State University, 1999 Aberdeen, South Dakota 7'x4'x4' wood
North Dakota State University 1999, 3'x8'x3' wood Fargo, North Dakota
Mary Ann Liegh Block Museum of Art, Northwestern University, 1999 Evanston, IL ( Print Collection) 2000
*Buena Vista University 2000 'Plato' 12'x10'x18', painted steel and ferroconcrete
City of North Lake, IL 2001 'Prairie Fault' (on loan) 9'x16'x18' painted steel and ferroconcrete
*Mid-America Group , 2005, Northpark Drive Streetscape, Urdandale, IA 'Hills, Fields, Wind, and Rain' 15'x32'x66' , Corten steel and ferroconcrete
*Ryan Companies, U.S. Inc., Clive, IA, "Prairie Emergence" 22' x 12' x 15' painted steel and ferroconcrete
*Iowa State Bank, Urbandale, IA, "Falling Water" 5'x 5' x 6" Bronze
Iowa State Bank, Urbandale, IA, " Babbling Brook"
Allied Group, varies corporate offices of Allied Group, 'Ripple', 'Trout Stream', 'Man In The Moon', 'Shallow', 'Gust'. 'Swoop'
Arkansas Fine Arts Center, Little Rock, AR . 'Nest'
*City of Clinton Iowa, 'Rivers Edge' 2008


**POSTHUMOUSLY**
Bernice Garden, 2011, 6' x 6' x 6', Little Rock, AR 'Spring Flower' 2011
Henderson State University,2012, Arkadelphia, AR, 'Bronko'

Many Private Collections

* Commissions  ** Competitive commissions


**Gallery Affiliations:**

West Des Moines, Iowa -   Olson/Larsen Galleries,  Marlene Olson   515-277-6734
Kansas City, Missouri -   Sherry Leedy Contemporary Art,   Sherry Leedy  816-474-1919
Taylor's Contemporary Fine Arts Gallery, Hot Springs, AR  501-624-0516

Selected works on file: General Services, Washington D.C.
Publication: National Community Arts Program, National Endowment for the Arts

**Teaching:**
Adjunct Professor of Sculpture, Henderson State University, Arkadelphia, AR 2002-2011
Professor of Art, Buena Vista University, Storm Lake, Iowa, 1971-2001 (Professor Emeritus)
Sculpture Workshop: Kansas City Art Institute, Summer 1977
TA University of Oklahoma

**Exhibitions, Grants, and Honors Posthumously:**

2013    group show: Olson Larson Galleries, West DesMoines, IA
        "Along the Trail" Outdoor Sculpture Show, Clive, IA
        Solo show: Buena Vista University, Storm Lake, IA
        Group show: Retrospective, Arkadelphia Arts Center, Arkadelphia, AR

2012    Delta Show 54th Annual , Arkansas Arts Center
        "Art Tracks" Outdoor Sculpture Exhibition, Palestine, TX

**Exhibitions, Grants, and Honors:**

2011    Art On The Green, International Sculpture Exhibition (invitational), Kemp Center For The Arts, Wichita Falls, TX

2010    Delta Show   Arkansas art Center Little Rock AR
        solo: Henderson State University . Arkadelphia, AR

2009    Sculpture Show Case   Hot Springs, AR
        Faculty Show, Henderson State University, Arkadelphia, AR

2008    Commission :City of Clinton Iowa, 'Rivers Edge' 12'X28'X22"

2007    Delta Exhibition   Arkansas Art Center   Little Rock, AR - received  Delta Award

2005    group show: Olson/Larson Galleries  West DesMoines, IA
        Faculty Show   Henderson State University, Arkadelphia, AR

2004    solo: Olson/Larson Galleries  West DesMoines, IA

2003    group show: Taylors Contemporanea,  Hot Springs, IA x

2002    solo: Olson Larson Galleries    West DesMoines,  IA
        Faculty Show – Henderson State University,   Arkadelphia, AR

2001    'Pier Walk 2001' Maquette Exhibition, Daley Center, Chicago, IL  March
        Gallery Night, Olson Larsen Gallery, West DesMoines, IA, April
        'Pier Walk 2001'Navy Pier, Chicago, IL , May 4-Oct 7
        Honorary Doctorate in Fine Arts , Buena Vista University

2000    'Numinous  Numeral MM' BAAC Gallery, Barrington, IL
        'Buena Vista University Faculty Exhibition', NICC Mason City, IA
        'Group Show', Olson Larsen Galleries, West DesMoines, IA

1999    Guest artist North Dakota State University, Fargo ND

solo: Northern Galleries, Northern State University, Aberdeen, S.D. Guest Artist
Artist in residence   Suburban Art Center, Highland Park IL
'Iowa Artist 1999' Des Monies Art Center ( juried)
New Work. Olson-Larsen Galleries. Des Monies, March 12th-April 10
Artist in residence Sioux City Art Center ( Jan. 4-15)
'The Maquette Exhibition for Pier Walk 99' Chicago's International Sculpture  Exhibition.
   Vedanta Gallery ,Chicago (Jan 15- Feb 13)

1998    solo - Peru State College, Peru Nebraska, November
solo ' New wood sculpture by Mac Hornecker' University of South Dakota, October
Buena Vista University Art Faculty Exhibition, Witter Gallery Storm Lake, IA. Feb.
1998 Personal Sightings III. Blanden Memorial  Art Museum, Fort Dodge IA. (juried)
'Art around the Corner' Sculpture exhibition, City of Ames IA (juried)
Hearst Center for the Arts, Cedar falls IA. Sculpture Garden Competition, (juried)
"Iowa Artist 98" Des Moines Art Center, (curator- Deborah Leventon)

1997    Commission - Hotel Pattee,  Perry Ia. 'Prairie Markers'  25'x60'x6' Ferro-Concrete
'Iowa Artist 97' Des Moines Art Center, Des Moines Ia.
solo - Sioux City Art Center, Sioux City Iowa
'Installation-Dewane Hughes, Jennifer Torres, Mac Hornecker' Wichita Center for the  Arts, Wichita. KS.

1996    Commission  - Employers Mutual Company  'Prairie Win'" , 50'x30'x10',  welded steel
'Proposals by Artists' concepts, drawings, Maquettes ( Invitational) Bellevue University
'New works by Paul Sierra and Mac Hornecker' Gallery 72, Omaha, NE, April
'Assemblage and Sculpture' Group show Olson/Larsen Galleries, Des Moines,      IA, March
'Iowa Artist 9' Des Moines Art Center (curated)

1995    'Alumni Select' (invitational) University of South Dakota
'Iowa Artist 1995' Des Moines Art Center (curated)
'Summer Arts XVIII' (Juried), University of South Dakota, Vermillion, SD
'The 45th Annual Quad-State' (Juried), Exhibition, (merit award) Quincy Art Center, Quincy, IL
 Solo:  Mount Mercy College, Cedar Rapids, IA
Guest Artist: Kentucky Wesleyan College, Owensboro, KY

1994 'Iowa Visions of Color' Invitational Iowa State University, Ames IA, Jan
    '15th Anniversary Exhibition'" Olson/Larsen Galleries, Des Moines, IA, April
    'New Work'   Mac Hornecker Olson/Larsen Galleries, Des Moines, IA, Sept
    Solo: ' Mac Hornecker Sculpture' Graceland College. Lamoni, IA, October
    Guest artist:  Kansas City Art Institute

1993 'Small Works' group show, Olson/Larsen Galleries, Des Moines, IA, December
    Solo:  Cox Gallery, Drury College, Springfield, MO, September
    Solo:  Waldorf College, Forest City, IA, September
    'Heartland National Arts Festival' Lenexa KS, (award) June
    Sculpture by Mac Hornecker, Olson-Larsen Galleries, Des Moines, IA, March
    'Salon D'January, 27 Artist' Gallery 72, Omaha, NE, January

Guest Artist: Northwest Missouri State, MO, Pittsburg State, KS, Drury
College, MO, University of Oklahoma, OK - University of Texas, Arlington, TX - and Wichita State, Wichita, KS

1992 Juror: Northwest Iowa High School Show, Witter Gallery, Storm Lake, IA
    Juror: Drake University All Student Show, Des Moines, IA
    Travel: Europe-Amsterdam-Klon-Munich-Rome-Pompei-Florence-Pisa-Paris-Geneva-London
    'Iowa Artist 1992' Des Moines Art Center -Curated by Holiday T. Day
    'Omaha Opera Invitational' Gallery 72, Omaha, NE
    'Sculptors that Draw' Invitational - Northwest Missouri State U. Maryville, MO

1991 Solo: 'Drawings and Sculpture by Mac Hornecker' Witter Gallery Storm Lake, IA, September
    Invitational: 'College Faculty Exhibit' Polk County Heritage Gallery, Des Moines, IA, September
    'Iowa Artist 1991' Des Moines Art Center - Curated by Sherry Cromwell-Lacy, September

1990 Solo: Charles H. MacNider Museum, Mason City, IA, Oct-Nov, Sculpture
    Olson/Larsen Galleries, West Des Moines, IA - Feb, Sculpture
    Olson/Larsen Galleries, West Des Moines, IA - June, Drawings
    International Sculpture 90, Washington, DC -Community exhibition- twenty
    sculpture Carega Foxley Leach Gallery (sponsor)
    One of three finalists, National competition- U232 Monument, Sioux City, IA

1989 'Earth Remembered' (Invitational), The Hook Gallery, Brooklyn, NY, April
    'Landscape: European and American Perspective' (invitational), Carega Foxley Leach Gallery.
    Washington, D.C. April
    Iowa Arts Council Juries/Slide bank and one of 12 Iowa artists-Public Arts Division
    'Paper and Objects' Drake University, Des Moines, IA

1988 Travel: China - Jan  Mexico - March
    Juror: South Dakota Sculpture Invitational Exhibition, 1988
    Solo: Olson/Larsen Gallery - Oct.
    Faculty Choice Invitational, University of South Dakota, October

# INDEX OF WORKS

| Page | |
|---|---|
| 78, 79 | Airbrush drawings of sculpture ideas |
| 88 | Aligned Landscape  14' x 34' x 10'  Corten steel and concrete, Northwestern University Orange City, IA  1980 |
| 144 | Babbling Brook  32" x 48" x 16"  Bronze, Iowa State Bank, Urbandale, IA |
| 114 | Bronko  7' x 14' x 7' steel and ferroconcrete  Henderson State University, Arkadelphia, AR |
| 95 | Buena Vista period sculpture maquettes- untitled |
| 91 | Buttress  10' x 5' x 5' steel and ferroconcrete  1985 |
| 107 | Caution to the Wind  34" x 72" x 32"  Mahogany wood, PA College of Optometry, Elkin Park, PA |
| 80, 82 | Drawings of ideas for sculpture |
| 158,161 | Drawings |
| 92 | Do-Dah Dancer  6' x 4' x 7'  steel and ferroconcrete  1987 |
| 112 | El Nino  8' x 7' x 14'     steel and ferroconcrete 1998 |
| 145 | Falling Water  5' x 5' x 6'   Bronze , Iowa State Bank, Urbandale, IA |
| 94 | Getty 8' x 6' x 8' steel and ferroconcrete  1996 |
| 141 | Gust  35" x 25" x 19" Bronze,  Allied Group corporate offices |
| 109 | Hammer  33" x 31" x 9"  wood oak and walnut |
| 139 | Hills, Fields, Wind, and Rain  15' x 22' x 26'  Corten and ferroconcrete, Northpark, Business Center, Urbandale, IA |
| 108 | Hoopdi Do  6' x 6' x 3'  pine wood |
| 151 | Hurricane  9' x 7' x 6' steel and ferroconcrete 2009 |
| 93 | Ice  8' x 6' x 3'  steel and ferroconcrete  11994 |
| 52-56 | Kansas City Art Institute Works, all untitled |
| 93 | Loess  6' x 5' x 9' steel and ferroconcrete  1995 |
| 84, 167 | MO Bluff  9' x 8' x 52' steel, concrete, and rock , City of Sheldon, MO 1977 |
| 89 | MO River  9' x 16' x 18'  corten steel, rock, concrete  Bellevue College, Bellevue, NB  1984 |
| 142 | Mountain Breeze  29' x 36' x 13'  Bronze |
| 154 | Mountain Draft  7' x 7' x 3'  welded steel |
| 143 | Mountain Spring  20" x 43" x 15"  Bronze, private collector |
| 126 | Plato  12' x 10' x 8' steel and ferroconcrete  Buena Vista University, Storm Lake 2000 |
| 87 | Prairie Bluff  32' x 9' x 10'  steel, concrete,, rock  South Dakota Memorial Art Center, Brookings , SD  1979 |
| 152 | Prairie Breeze  6' x 9' 6' welded steel and ferroconcrete |
| 147- 148 | Prairie Emergence  22' x 12' x 15' steel and ferroconcrete, Marketplace Mall, Clive, IA 2006 |

| | |
|---|---|
| 127 | Prairie Fault  9' x 16' x 8'  steel and ferroconcrete,  2001 |
| 157 | Prairie Flush  6' x 7' x 4  welded steel   2010 |
| 104 | Prairie Markers  ferroconcrete   Hotel Pattee,  Perry, IA 1997 |
| 102, 103 | Prairie Wind   15' x 30' x 15'  welded steel, Employers Mutual Company, DesMoines,IA 1996 |
| 97, 98 | River  12' x 50' x 12'  welded steel , Farm Bureau of Iowa, Urbandale, IA  1989 |
| 150 | River's Edge  12' x 28' x 22'  steel and ferroconcrete,  City of Clinton, IA  2008 |
| 90 | Rocket  4' x 6' x 7'  steel and ferroconcrete  1988 |
| 113 | Snail   8' x 8' x 14'  steel and ferroconcrete,  1998 |
| 92 | Splash  10' x 6' x 7'  steel and ferroconcrete,  1992 |
| 153 | Spring Flower   6' x 6'x 6'  steel and ferroconcrete, Bernice Garden, Little Rock, AR   2008 |
| 91 | Squeeze  20' x 10' x 6'  steel and ferroconcrete 1985 |
| 111 | Time Out, wood, 1999 |
| 105 | Tornado Struck  84" x 38" x 12"  Hotel Pattee,  Perry, IA 1997 |
| 140 | Trout Stream  33" x 33" x 39"  Bronze, Allied Group corporate offices |
| 62-64 | University of Oklahoma works, untitled |
| 110 | Outside the Loop, wood, 1999 |
| 105 | Up The Creek.  51' x 38" x 16"  wood , Hotel Pattee,  Perry, IA 1997 |
| 86 | Yellow One   7' x 16' x 12'  steel , Pacesetter, Omaha  (business closed so donated piece  to Buena Vista) 1977 |
| 106 | Wood Garden, wood, 1997  12' x 12' x 12' |

Made in the USA
Lexington, KY
29 July 2015